Lecture Notes in
Computer Science

ecture Notes in Computer Science

Lecture Notes in Computer Science

Edited by G. Goos and J. Hartmanis

96

James L. Peterson

Computer Programs for Spelling Correction:

An Experiment in Program Design

Springer-Verlag
Berlin Heidelberg NewYork 1980

Author

James L. Peterson
The Department of Computer Sciences
The University of Texas
Austin, Texas 78712/USA

AMS Subject Classifications (1979): 68 A 30
CR Subject Classifications (1974): 5.2, 3.42

ISBN 3-540-10259-0 Springer-Verlag Berlin Heidelberg New York
ISBN 0-387-10259-0 Springer-Verlag New York Heidelberg Berlin

PREFACE

"Anyone who can spell in English can't be very bright."

– George Bernard Shaw

The automatic detection and correction of spelling errors by computers has been a subject of interest for a long time. (Our literature search revealed work as early as 1957.) There have been several papers investigating various algorithms and showing their application to various tasks, generally data entry. Now, however, with the increased interest in computer based text processing (word processing) and the storage of large amounts of textual information in computers (data bases), we suggest that spelling correction will become commonplace. This volume brings together the diverse and scattered work on this topic and shows how it can be applied to create a real general purpose spelling corrector.

The theory behind spelling error detection and correction is only one of the considerations of this volume, however. More generally, we consider the design of the program to implement that theory. This work is an *experiment in program design*. Our objective is to demonstrate the application of modern program design principles on a large real (non-toy) program. The approach taken is:

1. A complete literature search provides the background information upon which our program will be based, introducing the problems and solutions which have been considered before.

2. Using our new familiarity with the subject, a complete, top–down program design will be created.

3. Finally, the design will be implemented by converting it into working code. The complete working program is given in Appendix III.

The purpose of this project is as much to investigate and demonstrate modern programming principles as to produce a spelling corrector. We feel that this project can be used as an example of the design of a large program. As such, it is suitable for study.

Consider using this volume in the classroom. The topic appeals to students; it is new, modern and has the appearance of intelligence. The simplest spelling error detector is an exercise in data structures, but it can be expanded and developed to illustrate many topics (disk I/0, interactive programming, data structures, performance, design, ...). Our experience has shown that it can be a very satisfactory programming project. Combining such a project with the reading of this volume provides both the experience and the example needed to motivate modern programming principles.

The program of Appendix III is available in machine readable form from the author (for a minimal cost to cover the computer time for preparing a copy of the program and shipping charges) for educational purposes.

James L. Peterson
Department of Computer Sciences
The University of Texas at Austin
Austin, Texas 78712

Acknowledgements – Discussions with William B. Ackerman, Robert Amsler, Michael Conner and Leigh Power helped to understand the problems of spelling programs. Jeanne Peterson assisted with proofreading and defining the style of this volume. Art Rinn, Emmett Griner, Mark McCulloch, Barney McCartney and the staff of Texas Student Publications aided in the preparation of the typeset copy. I greatly appreciate their help and time.

TABLE OF CONTENTS

Part I Background

Part II Design of a Spelling Program

PART I

Background

1.0   Introduction

Computers can assist in the production of documents in many ways. Formatting and editing can be consistently applied in a document, producing a high quality document. Appropriate software can be devised to improve the appearance of output on any output device, including typewriters and line printers. Use of sophisticated output devices, such as computer driven phototypesetters, or xerographic or electrostatic printers, can produce documents of outstanding quality.

Computers are being extensively used for document preparation. The systems used are typically a time-shared computer system (such as a DEC-10 or PDP-11 UNIX system) with their file systems, text editors and text formatting programs. The author can enter the document directly on-line with the text editor, storing it in the computer's file system. The document is stored with formatting commands indicating appropriate margins, spacing, paging, indenting, and so on. The text formatter interprets this file to produce an output file suitable for printing. The text file can be quickly modified using a text editor and a new version of the document produced as necessary. The text editor is generally an interactive program, while the formatter is more often a batch program.

This method of document preparation was originally used only by computer science researchers, but the advantages of computer assisted document handling have created a market for *word processing* systems. This market will grow as more and more groups apply computers to improve their document preparation.

Once this mode of document preparation is adopted, however, several other operations on the text files other than editing and formatting become possible. Of particular interest here is the possibility of analyzing documents for *spelling errors*. Several systems have programs which can analyze a text file for potential spelling errors, often pointing out probable correct spellings. This is a fairly recent form of text processing, but its potential is clear to those who have used spelling programs. We expect spelling programs to be a standard part of all future text processing systems.

There are two types of spelling programs: *spelling checkers* and *spelling correctors*. The problem for a spelling checker is quite simple: Given an input file of text, identify those words which are incorrectly spelled. A spelling corrector both detects misspelled words and tries to determine the most likely correctly spelled word which was meant. This problem has elements of pattern recognition and coding theory. A solution is possible only because of the rather great redundancy in the English language.

Each word can be thought of as a point in a multi–dimensional space of letter sequences. Not all letter sequences are words, and the spelling checker must classify each candidate word from the input (called a *token*) as a correctly spelled word or not. We want to minimize errors in classification, both errors of Type I (saying a correctly spelled word is incorrect) and errors of Type II (saying an incorrectly spelled word is correct). In spelling correction, we want to also identify the correct spelling. This involves a search of the word space to select the nearest neighbor(s) of the incorrectly spelled word as the candidates for correct spelling. (This view of words in a multi–dimensional space can lead to peculiar representations of words such as in [Giangardella, *et al* 1967] in which each word is represented as a vector in a 2–dimensional space.)

Spelling errors can be introduced into a file in many ways. The following three ways are probably the most important.

Author ignorance of correct spelling. These errors would lead to consistent misspellings, probably related to the differences between how a word sounds and how it is spelled.

Typographical errors when text is keyboarded. These errors would be less consistent but perhaps more predictable, since they would be related to the position of keys on the keyboard, and probably would result for specific errors in finger movements. Studies have shown that large data bases may have significant errors introduced in keyboarding [Bourne 1977].

Transmission and storage errors within the computer system. These errors would be related to the specific encoding and transmission mechanisms used. Some early work in spelling correction was aimed at the specific problem of optical character recognition (OCR) input [Bledsoe and Browning 1959; Harmon 1962; Vossler and Branston 1964; Carlson 1966] and the recognition of Morse code [McElwain and Evans 1962].

Some checking or correcting algorithms may be better for some types of errors.

The original motivation for research on spellers was to correct errors in data entry. Hence much of the early work was directed at finding and correcting errors resulting from specific input devices in specific contexts. For example, Davidson [1962] was concerned with finding the (potentially misspelled) names of passengers for a specific airline flight. Either (or both) name (in the passenger list or the query) might be misspelled. Similarly, Carlson [1966] was concerned with names and places in a genealogical data base. Freeman [1963] was working only with variable names and keywords in the CORC programming language while McElwain and Evans [1962] were concerned with improving the output of a system to recognize Morse code. Each of these projects considered the spelling problem as only one aspect of a larger problem, and not as a separate software tool on its own.

Similarly, many academic studies have been on the general problem of string matching and correction algorithms [Damerau 1964; Alberga 1967; Riseman and Ehrich 1971; Wagner and Fisher 1974; Riseman and Hanson 1974; Lowrance and Wagner 1975], but not with the aim of producing a working spelling program for general text.

Recently, however, several spelling checkers have been written for the sole purpose of checking arbitrary text files. Research on spelling correction extends back to 1957, but the first spelling checker written as an application program (rather than a research experiment) appears to have been SPELL for the DEC-10, written by Ralph Gorin at Stanford in 1971. This program, and its revisions, are widely distributed today on both DEC-10 and DEC-20 computer systems.

The UNIX operating system provides two spelling checkers: TYPO and SPELL. These are different approaches to the same problem, as will be discussed later.

Another spelling checker has been written for IBM/360 and IBM/370 systems and is in use at the IBM Thomas J. Watson Research Center at Yorktown Heights.

These programs have been investigated; this volume reports on the operation of these programs: how they work and the resulting advantages and disadvantages. As a result, we illustrate how a spelling checker can be written for other systems, using existing software technology.

2.0   Token Lists

The simplest form of computer assistance in detecting spelling errors is a program which simply lists all distinct tokens in the input document. This requires a person to scan the list, identifying any misspellings. A program of this sort is a simple exercise and should be easy to write.

Even at this point, however, significant decisions must be made about what is a potential word (token). A word is a sequence of *letters*, separated by *delimiters*. Delimiters include blanks and special characters, such as commas, periods, colons, and so on. In most cases, the classification of a character as a letter or a delimiter is clear, but careful thought should be given to the interpretation of numbers, hyphens, and apostrophes.

Tokens which include numbers are often ignored by spelling checkers. This includes both tokens which are totally numbers ("1978", "10", and so on), and tokens which are part number and part letter ("3M", "IBM360", "R2D2", and so on). Whether these sorts of tokens should be considered by a speller might be best left as an option to be selected by the user.

Hyphens are generally considered delimiters; each part of the hyphenated token is considered a separate token. This follows from the normal use of a hyphen to construct compound words (such as "German-American", "great-grandmother", "four-footed", and so on). The use of hyphens for hyphenation at the end of a line is best not allowed in the input to a spelling checker, since it should be well known that it is not possible in general to undo such hyphenation correctly.

Apostrophes are generally considered to be letters for the purpose of spelling correction. This is because of their use as an indicator of omitted letters (as in "don't", "I'd", and so on), and possessives ("King's", "John's", and so on). An apostrophe at the beginning or end of a token might be considered a delimiter, since they are sometimes used as quote markers (as in: "the token 'ten' ..."), but plural possessives also have apostrophes at the ends of words ("kids'").

Another concern is for the *case* of letters in a token. Most frequently all letters will be in lower case, although the first letter is capitalized at the start of a sentence. Since "the" is normally considered the same word as "The", most spellers map all letters into one case (upper or lower) for analysis. A flag may be associated with the token to allow proper capitalization for spelling correctors, since we want the capitalization of corrected tokens to match the capitalization of the input token. Thus "amung" should be corrected to "among" while "Amung" is corrected to "Among".

The case problem is actually more complex than this because of the existence of words, particularly in computer literature, which are strictly upper case (such as "FORTRAN", "IBM", and so on) and the widespread use of acronyms ("GCD", "CPU", and so on) which are typically upper case. Should "fortran" or "ibm" be considered misspellings or separate words from their upper case equivalents? (This is especially true in languages such as German where use of incorrect upper or lower case is considered a spelling error.) What should be the cases of the letters used to correct an input token such as "aMunG"? These problems are minor but need thought for spelling correctors. Spelling checkers need only report that "aMunG" is not a correctly spelled token in any case; this allows all tokens to be mapped into a uniform case for checking.

A separate problem is a possible decision that tokens which consist solely of upper case characters should (optionally) not even be considered by a spelling corrector since they most likely will be proper names, variable names, or acronyms, none of which would typically be understood by a spelling program anyway.

Once these decisions are made, it is relatively straightforward to write a program to create a list of all distinct tokens. The basic algorithm is:

Initialize. Get the name of the input file and the output file for the list, open them, and set all variables to their initial state.

Loop. While there are still tokens in the input file, get the next token, and enter it into an internal table of tokens.

To enter the token, first search to see if it is already in the table. If not, then add it to the table.

Print. When all tokens have been read from the input file, print the table and stop.

The key to this program is obviously its internal table of tokens. We need to be able to quickly search the table and find a token if it exists in the table, or determine that it is not in the table. We also need to be able to add new tokens to the table. Note that we need not delete tokens from the table. The speed of the program is most dependent on the search time. A hashing table approach would seem the most reasonable data structure for the table (more on this later).

The table would be most useful if it were *sorted*. Sorting can be either alphabetically or by frequency. Attaching a frequency count to each table entry provides a count of the number of uses of each token. This can speed the search of the table by searching higher frequency items first (a self–modifying table structure) and also may give help in determining misspellings. Typographical errors are generally not repeated, and so tokens typed incorrectly will tend to have very low frequency. Any token with low frequency is thus suspect. Consistent misspellings (due to the author not knowing the correct spelling) are not as easily found by this technique.

3.0   TYPO

An extension of this idea is the basis of the TYPO program on UNIX [Morris and Cherry 1975; McMahon, *et al* 1978]. This program resulted from research on the frequency of two–letter pairs (*digrams*) and three–letter triples (*trigrams*) in English text. If there are 28 letters (alphabetic, blank, and apostrophe) then there are 28^2 (= 784) digrams and 28^3 (= 21,952) trigrams. However, the frequency of these digrams and trigrams varies greatly, with many being extremely rare. Typically, in a large sample of text, only 550 digrams (70%) and 5000 trigrams (25%) actually occur. If a token contains several very rare digrams or trigrams, it is potentially misspelled.

The use of digrams and trigrams to both detect probable spelling errors and in- dicate probable corrections has been one of the most popular techniques in the literature [Harmon 1962; McElwain and Evans 1962; Vossler and Branston 1964; Carlson 1966; Cornew 1968; Riseman and Ehrich 1971; Riseman and Hanson 1974; Morris and Cherry 1975; McMahon, *et al* 1978].

TYPO computes the actual frequency of digrams and trigrams in the input text and a list of the distinct tokens in the text. Then for each distinct token, an *index of peculiarity* is computed. The index for a token is the root-mean-square of the indices for each trigram of the token. The index for a trigram xyz given digram and trigram frequencies $f(xy)$, $f(yz)$ and $f(xyz)$ is $[log(f(xy)-1) + log(f(yz)-1)]/2 - log(f(xyz)-1)$. (The *log* of zero is defined as -10 for this computation.) This index is a statistical measure of the probability that the trigram xyz was produced by the same source that produced the rest of the text.

The index of peculiarity measures how unlikely the token is in the context of the rest of the text. The output of TYPO is a list of tokens, sorted by index of peculiarity. Experience indicates that misspelled tokens tend to have high indices of peculiarity, and hence appear towards the front of the list. Errors tend to be found since (a) misspelled words are found quickly at the beginning of the list (motivating the author to continue looking), and (b) the list is relatively short. In a document of ten thousand tokens only approximately 1500 distinct tokens occur. This number is further reduced in TYPO by comparing each token with a list of over 2500 common words. If the token occurs in this list, it is known to be correct and is not output by TYPO. This simple process will typically eliminate half of the distinct input tokens, producing a much shorter list to be inspected by the author as potential misspellings.

4.0   Dictionary Look-up

The use of an external list (a *dictionary*) of correctly spelled words is the next level of sophistication in spelling checkers. The spelling checker algorithm using a dictionary is:

Initialize.

Build List. Construct a list of all distinct tokens in the input file.

Search. Look up each token of the list in the dictionary.

If the token is in the dictionary, it is correctly spelled.

If the token is not in the dictionary, it is not known to be correctly spelled, and is put on the output list for the user's attention.

Print. Print the list of tokens which were not found in the dictionary.

If the list of input tokens and the dictionary are sorted, then only one pass through the list and dictionary is needed to check all input tokens, providing a very fast checker.

The major component of this algorithm is the dictionary. Several dictionaries exist in machine readable form, or one could sit and type one in. More practical would be to use the output of the spelling checker to create the dictionary. The output is a list of tokens which are not in the dictionary. Starting with a small dictionary, many correctly spelled but unknown words will be output by the checker. By deleting spelling errors and proper names from this list, we have a list of new words which can be added to the dictionary. Since both the old dictionary and the new words are sorted, a new dictionary can be easily created by merging the two.

The size of a reasonable dictionary can be estimated by the existence of books which simply list words, mainly for use in spelling by secretaries, such as [Leslie 1977]. A survey of local bookstores reveals such books with 20K, 20K, 35K and 40K words.

One must be careful not to produce too large a dictionary. A large dictionary may tend to include rare, archaic or obsolete words. The occurrence of these words in technical writing is most likely the result of a misspelling. Another problem with most large dictionaries is the tendency of incorrectly spelled words to creep into the dictionary. It is certainly neither interesting nor pleasant to manually verify the correct spelling of 100,000 words.

A dictionary of 10,000 words, particularly if produced by a small community of users, should be quite reasonable. Since the average word in English is about eight characters, this requires about 100K bytes of storage in the computer system. Hence, the dictionary will probably be shared among the users of the system. Controls will be needed on who may modify the dictionary.

The need for controls on the modification of the shared dictionary creates the need for a system *dictionary administrator*. The dictionary administrator would be responsible for maintaining the shared system dictionary. This involves the addition of new words (or words whose frequency of use suddenly increases) and the selective deletion of infrequently used words.

One approach to limiting the size of the system dictionary is to create multiple dictionaries, one for each major topic area. This leads naturally to the concept of a common base dictionary with multiple local dictionaries of special words specific to a given topic. When a particular file is to be checked, a temporary master dictionary is created by augmenting the common base with selected local dictionaries. These local dictionaries can be created and maintained by the dictionary administrator or by individual users to reflect their own vocabularies.

The algorithm mentioned above for dictionary look-up is a *batch* algorithm. It is essentially the algorithm used for the UNIX and IBM spelling programs. There are some problems with this approach. First, a substantial real-time wait may be required while the program is running. This can be quite annoying to a user at an interactive console. Second, the output list of misspelled and unknown tokens lacks context. It may be difficult to find some tokens in the text using some text editors due to differences in case (for editors which pay attention to upper/lower case) and search difficulties (the file may be quite large, and/or the misspelled token may be a commonly occurring substring in correctly spelled words).

5.0   Interactive Spelling Checkers

These problems can be easily corrected with an *interactive* spelling checker. An interactive checker uses the following basic algorithm.

Initialize. This may include asking the user for mode settings and the names of local dictionaries to be used.

Check. For each token of the input file, search the dictionary for it.

If the token is not in the dictionary, ask the user what to do about it.

This is the approach of the DEC–10 SPELL program.

5.1   *Modes of Operation*

Several *modes* of operation may be useful in an interactive checker. The interaction with the user may be *verbose* (for novice users) or *terse* (for experts who are familiar with the program). Local dictionaries of specialized terms may be temporarily added to the large shared system dictionary. A training mode (where all tokens not in the system dictionary are defined to be correctly spelled) may be useful for constructing such local dictionaries.

The options available to the user when an unknown token is found are determined by user needs. The following list indicates some possible options.

Replace. The unknown token is taken to be misspelled and should be replaced. The token is deleted from the input stream and a correctly spelled word is then requested from the user to be inserted in its place.

Replace and Remember. The unknown token is to be replaced by a user specified word, and all future uses of this token are also to be replaced by the new word.

Accept. The token is correct (in this context) and should be left alone.

Accept and Remember. The unknown token is correct and should be left alone. In addition, all future uses of this token are correct in this document and the user should not be asked about them again.

Edit. Enter an editing submode allowing the file to be arbitrarily modified in the local context of the token.

Use of a CRT as the terminal for interaction with the speller allows the spelling checker to display the context of an unknown token. At least the line in which the token is found should be displayed. On terminals with sufficient bandwidth and features, a larger context of several lines or an entire page could be displayed with the token emphasized by brightness, blinking, size or font.

5.2   The Dictionary

The performance of an interactive spelling checker is of great concern. The user is waiting for the checker and so the checker must be sufficiently fast to avoid frustrating the user. Also, unlike the batch checkers which need to look up each distinct token only once (and can sort these tokens to optimize the order of search), an interactive checker must look up each occurrence of a token in the order in which they are used. Thus, the interactive checker intrinsically must do more work.

(It would be possible to batch small portions, up to say a page, of the input file. A list of all distinct tokens on a page would be created and the dictionary searched for each token. Each token which was not found would be presented to the user. This is repeated for each page in the input file. The main problems are with response time and in keeping track of the context of each usage of a token for display.)

The structure of the dictionary is therefore of great importance. The dictionary structure must allow very fast searches. The "correct" structure must be determined for the configuration of the local computer system. Such factors as memory size, file access methods, and the existence of virtual memory can be significant factors determining appropriate data structures. If memory is large enough, the entire dictionary can be kept in memory making things much easier and faster. If this memory is virtual, as opposed to physical, however, the dictionary structure should be selected to minimize page faults while searching. If memory is too small, a two–layer structure is needed, keeping the most frequently referenced words in memory, while accessing the remainder with disk reads as necessary.

Many algorithms and data structures for text processing are affected by the properties of the English language. Several studies have created large computer files of text which can then be analyzed to determine the statistical properties of the language. The most commonly cited such collection is the Brown Corpus [Kucera and Francis 1967] created at Brown University. The Brown Corpus contains 1,014,-232 total tokens with 50,406 distinct words. The longest word is 44 characters, while 99% are 17 characters or less in length. The average word length is 8.1 characters. It is well known however that short words are used more frequently than long words. The ten most common words are "the", "of", "and", "to", "a", "in", "that", "is", "was", and "he". Because of this higher usage of shorter words, the average token length when weighted by frequency of use is only 4.7 characters, with 99% of the words being of 12 characters or less in length.

Knuth [1973] is a good source for different data structures and search strategies. Several different algorithms and their properties are considered. However, there is no "best" algorithm; each machine and each system makes different demands on the dictionary data structure. A few approaches are outlined below.

The DEC–10 SPELL program uses a hash chain table of 6760 entries. The hash function for a token is the first two letters (L1 and L2) and the length (WL) of the token (2, 3, ..., 10, 11 and over) as (L1*26 + L2) * 10 + $min(WL-2,9)$. Each hash table entry is a pointer to a chain of words all of which have the same first two letters and the same length. (This program assumes all tokens of length 1 are correctly spelled.)

Another suggested structure for the dictionary is based on *tries* [Knuth 1973; Partridge and James 1974; Muth and Tharp 1977]. A large tree structure represents the dictionary. The root of the tree branches to 26 different nodes, one for each of the possible first letters of words in the dictionary. Each of these nodes would branch according to the possible second letters, given the known first letter associated with the node. These new nodes branch on possible third letters, and so on. A special bit would indicate the possible ends of words. This structure is particularly appropriate for small computer systems in which a token must be compared with a dictionary entry one character at a time. To search for a token of WL characters requires following the tree WL levels down and checking the end–of–word bit.

Alternative structures are generally based on the frequency of use of words. It is known that usage is extremely variable, and a small number of words are used most often. Hence, we want to structure our search strategy so that the most common words are searched first. One suggestion [Sheil 1978] is for a *two–level search strategy*.

In the two–level search strategy, a given token would first be looked up in the small in–core table of most frequently used words. If the token is not in this table, a search would be made of a larger table of the remaining words. This larger table might be stored on secondary disk or drum storage, or in a separate part of virtual memory, requiring longer access and search times. If this table were on secondary storage, direct access to a particular block, which could be identified by an in–core index structure, would be most effective.

From the Brown Corpus, we can determine the following statistics for the percentage of tokens in normal English which would be found in a search of a table of the most common English words. The size of the table determines the percentage of tokens found. As the table size is doubled, a larger percentage of tokens are found.

Table Size	Percent Tokens Found	Gain
16	28.8	
32	36.0	7.2
64	43.2	7.2
128	49.6	6.4
256	55.8	6.2

Over half of the tokens in normal English result from a vocabulary of only 168 words. A table of this size can easily be stored in memory. A good search strategy can be designed to speed search of this small table. For example, Knuth [1973] gives a hashing algorithm which results in only one comparison to identify any of the 31 most frequently used words in English (35.7% of all tokens).

Another improvement in search time can be made by noticing that the total number of distinct tokens in a document tends to be small to moderate (1500 for a 10,000 word document) and often uses words of particular interest to the specific subject area. This means that for each specific document, there exists a (small) table of words which occur frequently in that document (but not in normal English). Thus, it is wise to build another table of words which have been used in this specific document. This three–table structure would be searched by:

First, search the small table of most common English words.

Next, search the table of words which have already been used in this document.

Finally, search the large list of the remaining words in the main dictionary. If a word is found at this level, add it to the table of words for this document.

Distinct data structures may be appropriate for these three tables since they exhibit the following different properties.

Most common English words — static, small (100–200).

Document specific words — dynamic, small to moderate (1000–2000).

Secondary storage dictionary — static, very large (10,000–100,000).

Separate search strategies are also appropriate.

(You may recognize the latter two data structures as similar to a paging or segmentation scheme. Notice that even if the underlying computer system provides a virtual memory by such a memory management scheme, this data structure will provide improved locality and hence a lower fault rate.)

6.0 Spelling Correction

An interactive spelling checker can also be helpful in spelling correction. In the simplest case, the checker remembers all tokens which the user indicates should be replaced, and the words with which they are to be replaced. After the first such replacement, future occurrences of the misspelled token can be automatically corrected. (This feature might be undesirable in some instances.)

A similar approach is to include in the dictionary common misspellings with an indication of the correct spelling. Thus "greatfully" would be tagged as a misspelling of "gratefully" and "prehaps" as a misspelling of "perhaps". This approach has not been included in any current spellers. Most likely this is because of the lack of an obvious source of known misspellings and the probable low frequency of even common misspellings.

Another reason for not storing common misspellings is that most misspellings can be generated from correct spellings by a few simple rules. Damerau [1964] indicates that 80% of all spelling errors are the result of:

1. transposition of two letters

2. one letter extra

3. one letter missing

4. one letter wrong

These four rules are the basis of the correction portion of the DEC-10 spelling corrector. The basic algorithm for correction is as follows.

For each token which is not found in the dictionary, construct a list of all words which could produce this token by one of the above rules. These are candidate spellings.

If the list has exactly one candidate, guess that word, and ask the user if that word is the correct spelling.

If the list has several words, indicate to the user that you have a list of candidates. The user may ask to see the list and select one as the correct word, or may indicate one of the normal options of replace, replace and remember, accept, accept and remember, or edit.

The candidate list is formed by multiple searches of the dictionary. Transpositions can be detected by transposing each pair of adjacent characters in the token, one at a time, and searching for the resulting token in the dictionary. If the resulting token is found, it is a candidate and is added to the list. For a token of WL characters, this requires $WL-1$ searches of the dictionary. Checking for one extra letter requires deleting each character in the token, one at a time, and searching for the resulting tokens. This requires an additional WL searches. Note that most tokens are short (five characters on average) so this need not be expensive. (On the other hand, no statistics are available for the lengths of misspelled words, so this may be a false comfort.)

The remaining two types of errors (one missing letter and one wrong letter) are more expensive to search for. Two strategies are possible. The comparison operation for comparing two words can be defined to include a special *match-any* character which will match any character. This means that a search for a missing last letter could be done by appending the special *match-any* character and searching. The characteristics of this type of search are more complex than a simple bit-wise compare and so will probably take more time per compare. Considering the critical nature of the compare for performance, two separate searches may be needed: with and without the *match-any* character feature. Also it should be noted that a search with a *match-any* character feature cannot stop when the first word match is found, but must continue since many words may match the token. This approach requires $WL+1$ searches for a missing letter error and WL searches for a wrong letter error.

A second approach is to substitute each potential character in each character position and search normally. If there are N potential characters (N approximately 27 depending on the classification of the apostrophe and similar characters), then a missing letter error requires $N * (WL+1)$ searches and a wrong letter $N*WL$ searches.

A specific dictionary structure may allow improvements on the number and type of searches required. The DEC-10 SPELL program separates the dictionary into 6760 chains by the first two letters and length. For a token of length WL, candidate spellings for one letter wrong and transposition errors are of the same length, candidates for one letter extra errors are of length $WL-1$, and one letter missing candidates are of length $WL+1$. This considerably shortens the number of chains which must be searched. The search strategy is best described by quoting from the comments of the program itself.

"There are four kinds of errors that the program attempts to correct:

one wrong letter.
one missing letter.
one extra letter.
two transposed letters.

For a wrong letter in the third or subsequent character, all words that are candidates must exist on the same chain that the suspect token hashes to. Hence, each entry on that chain is inspected to determine if the suspect differs from the entry by exactly one character. This is accomplished by an exclusive-or (XOR) between the suspect and the dictionary. Then a JFFO instruction selects the first nonzero byte in the XOR. This byte is zeroed and if the result is all zero then the dictionary word differs from the suspect in only one letter. All such words are listed at CANDBF, where they can be inspected later. For a wrong letter in the first or second character, the program tries varying the second letter through all 26 possible values, searching for an exact match. Then all 26 possible values of the first letter are tried, after setting the second letter to its original value. This means that 52 more chains are searched for possible matches. To correct transposed letters, all combinations of transposed letters are tried. There are only $WL-1$ such combinations, so it is fairly cheap to do that. To correct one extra letter, WL copies of the token are made, each with some letter removed.

Each of these is looked up in the dictionary. This takes WL searches. To correct one missing letter, $WL+1$ copies of the token are made, each time inserting a null character in a new position in the suspect. The null character is never part of any word, so the suspect token augmented by an embedded null can be thought of as a word with one wrong letter (the null). Then the algorithm for matching one wrong letter is used. If the first character is omitted, all 26 possible first characters are tried. Also, 26 more tokens are formed by varying the second character in case that had been omitted."

Counting, we find that a total of $3*WL+103$ chains must be searched, with WL such chain searches requiring a special algorithm to look for (exactly) one wrong character. Remember that the dictionary (of say 100,000 words) is split into 6760 chains, so a chain search looks at only on the order of 5 to 50 words. For a token of 8 characters this might mean 3000 comparisons.

Spelling correction is certainly not cheap. (But on the other hand, it is not prohibitively expensive nor is it needed for the majority of tokens, only those few which are not found in the dictionary.)

Other correction algorithms have been suggested. One theoretically pleasing suggestion [Alberga 1967] is to determine the lengths of common substrings in a token and a dictionary word. This can be used to determine an *index of matching*. The index of matching can be thought of as the probability that the token resulted from a misspelling of the dictionary word. The word with the highest probability can be selected as the most likely correct spelling. This would seem to be a very expensive algorithm.

Similar algorithms have been investigated by Wagner and Fischer [1974] and Lowrance and Wagner [1975].

Notice that additional information can often be used to increase correction accuracy or speed. One important source of additional information is the source of possible errors. For example, errors introduced by OCR input devices are only the substitution of one letter for another; characters are never inserted or deleted by the OCR reader. In addition it is possible to create a *confusion matrix* giving the probability $p_{i,j}$ of reading a character i when the correct character is j. This confusion matrix can be used to indicate which characters should be considered when an input letter is to be corrected. In a more general system, digram and trigram frequencies could be used to limit the number of alternative spellings which must be considered.

The layout of the standard typewriter keyboard may be of use in correcting errors introduced in keyboarding text into a system.

Another suggested technique attacks the problem of words which the original author did not know how to spell correctly. The misspellings in this case are often based on how the word sounds. Thus it has been suggested that tokens should be converted to a standard phonetic spelling which would be used to find similarly sounding words in the dictionary. This would help correct such apparent double errors as using "f" for "ph" or "k" for "qu".

On the other hand, correction based upon the four rules used by the DEC–10 SPELL program is quite successful and relatively cheap, leaving the more difficult corrections to the user.

7.0   Affix Analysis

The major problem with an interactive speller is the size of the dictionary. For performance reasons, it is desirable to keep the dictionary in memory if at all possible. Thus serious thought has gone into means of reducing the size of the dictionary. The Brown Corpus had 50,406 distinct words, but over half were used only once or twice. A dictionary of 8000 words would represent 90% of the words used in the Brown Corpus; 16,000 words would yield 95%.

A major reduction may be possible however by considering common *affixes*. (An affix is either a *suffix* or a *prefix*.) Most plural nouns and verbs result from adding an "–s" to the end of the singular form. Other common suffixes include "–ly", "–ing", "–est", "–er", "–ed", "–ion" and so on. By removing these suffixes and storing only the root word, the dictionary can be significantly reduced in size. Similar approaches are possible for prefixes.

Two approaches are possible here. In the simplest case, each token is examined for a list of common affixes. These are removed if found. Hence any token ending in "–s", has the "–s" removed. (The order of search can assure that larger suffixes, like "–ness" are removed first.) Then the resulting token is looked for in the dictionary. If found, the token is judged correct. A major problem with this approach is that it does not catch misspelled tokens which are the result of correct affixes incorrectly applied to correct words, such as "implyed" or "fixs". This can allow a large number of misspelled tokens to escape detection.

The correct solution to this problem is to flag each word in the dictionary with its legal affixes. With this approach, the dictionary is first searched for the token. If the token is not found, it is examined for possible affixes. These are removed and the dictionary searched for the root word. If the root is found in the dictionary, its flags are examined to see that the particular affix removed is legal for this root.

The rules associated with affix removal can be quite complex. As an example, the following flags, and their interpretation are used in the DEC–10 SPELL program. These rules show how to add a suffix to a root word. Let α and β be "variables" that can stand for any letter. Upper case letters are constants. "..." stands for any string of zero or more letters.

"V" flag:

  ...E —> ...IVE
  ...α —> ...αIVE, if α is not E

"N" flag:

  ...E —> ...ION
  ...Y —> ...ICATION
  ...α —> ...αEN, if α is not E or Y.

"X" flag:

  ...E —> ...IONS
  ...Y —> ...ICATIONS
  ...α —> ...ENS, if α is not E or Y.

"H" flag:

  ...Y —> ...IETH
  ...α —> ...αTH, if α is not Y.

"Y" flag:

  ... —> ...LY

"G" lag:

  ...E —> ...ING
  ...α —> ...αING, if α is not E.

"J" flag:

  ...E —> ...INGS
  ...α —> ...αINGS, if α is not E.

"O" flag:

  ...E —> ...ED
  ...βY —> ...βIED, if β is not A, E, I, O, or U
  ...$\beta\alpha$ —> ...$\beta\alpha$ED, otherwise.

"T" flag:

  ...E —> ...EST
  ...βY —> ...βIEST, if β is not A, E, I, O, or U
  ...$\beta\alpha$ —> ...$\beta\alpha$EST, otherwise.

"R" flag:

  ...E —> ...ER
  ...βY —> ...βIER, if β is not A, E, I, O, or U
  ...$\beta\alpha$ —> ...$\beta\alpha$ER, otherwise.

"Z" flag:

  ...E —> ...ERS
  ...βY —> ...βIERS, if β is not A, E, I, O, or U
  ...$\beta\alpha$ —> ...$\beta\alpha$ERS, otherwise.

"S" flag:

$...\beta Y \longrightarrow ...\beta IES$, if β is not A, E, I, O, or U

$...\alpha \longrightarrow ...\alpha ES$, if α is S, X, Z, or H

$...\alpha \longrightarrow ...\alpha S$, otherwise.

"P" flag:

$...\beta Y \longrightarrow ...\beta INESS$, if β is not A, E, I, O, or U

$...\beta\alpha \longrightarrow ...\beta\alpha NESS$, otherwise.

Suffix removal requires the correct reversal of the above rules, showing how to produce a root and suffix from an input token. Similar rules must be defined for prefix removal.

The interaction of affix removal and spelling correction is not well understood, nor is iterated affix removal (removing several affixes).

Of the three known spelling checkers, each uses a different approach to affix analysis. The IBM speller uses no affix analysis, preferring a larger but simpler dictionary. The UNIX speller removes a few common suffixes and prefixes with no check for the legality of these affixes on the resulting root. Some of the DEC-10 SPELL programs maintain the flags listed above.

PART II

Design of a Spelling Program

8.0   Introduction

The literature search presented in Part I provides the background for our design of a spelling corrector. Our goal is to create an interactive spelling corrector program. This statement is the extent of our explicit specifications. Other specifications are implicit: good performance, ease of use, and so on, but we allow ourselves considerable flexibility at this time. In part this is because we wish to postpone specific decisions until they are absolutely necessary; in part this is because we cannot give a complete specification at this time. We do not know all of the decisions which will be necessary, nor the relative costs and benefits of our alternatives. In this respect, we must consider this project as research.

Several assumptions are made before we start our design. First, the goal is an *interactive spelling corrector design*. This design is machine independent and based on proper program structuring concepts. Therefore it can easily be implemented on any available system. The design is expressed in a Pascal-like language augmented in minor ways as necessary to correct any problems with the language. Remember the immediate purpose of this part is a *design*, not an implementation.

The design is top-down. This allows important functions, like dictionary look-up, creation of the list of guessed spellings, and so on, to be replaced by stubs to check out the high-level design, as necessary. Also, these low-level routines, which do most of the work, are those most likely to reflect machine dependencies, and hence should properly be left until last.

We begin by considering first the various files which are needed and then a coding convention for indicating user-selected options.

8.1   *Files*

At least four files are needed by the speller.

1. Interactive input (TTYI).

2. Interactive output (TTYO).

3. File to be checked (INPUT).

4. File to be produced (OUTPUT).

The TTYI and TTYO files are used to communicate with the user, both for the initial dialog and for subsequent interaction concerning potentially misspelled tokens. The OUTPUT is identical to the INPUT, except that identified misspellings are corrected, of course.

One additional file may also be necessary: a file for the dictionary. However, the dictionary may be core resident in some systems, and so we do not consider that now.

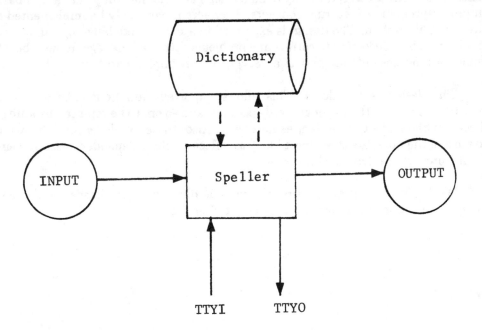

Figure 1. File structure for the spelling program.

Note that the TTYO file will be used for any and all error messages, so that a separate error file is not needed.

8.2   Modes

A program such as a speller can have many possible uses in many environments. However, for best use, this may require slightly different coding for some uses. These variations in apparent function can be controlled by various mode setting flags, such as:

* Quit mode: exit as soon as possible.

* Verbose mode: for new users, who may need lots of prompting.

* Terse mode: for users who need only minimal help or prompting.

* Various Display modes: see the section below on display.

* Training mode: several variants on this are possible, allowing the user to produce a local dictionary of words for a given document. For example:

    a. All tokens not in the dictionary can be assumed correctly spelled and put into a local dictionary. This local dictionary is then a list of all unique words in the INPUT file which are not in the master dictionary and reflects any special terms used.

    b. Same as in a., but with the master dictionary deleted first, so that the local dictionary produced lists *all* unique words in the INPUT file.

* Suffix or prefix analysis (or both) can be enabled or disabled for those systems which do such analysis.

* Retain mode: the speller can remember how a misspelled token was corrected and automatically use that correction if the misspelled token was encountered again, or not.

* Syntax modes: Words which are in special fonts, contain numbers, are all upper case, and so on can either be considered as tokens, to be checked, or not.

Other mode settings are also possible. These depend both upon the specific implementation and upon specific demands in given environments. Thus, we need to allow flexibility and variability here.

One proposal is an array of boolean flags. These flags each define two modes: the flag is on, or the flag is off. These mode flags can then be used throughout the speller as necessary. The flags can be an array as:

mode_type = (*terse, train, affix, ...*);
mode: **array** [*mode_type*] **of** *boolean* (* initially all off *);

Then a flag can be used as,

if *mode*[*terse*]
   then *write* (*TTYO*, '?')
   else begin
         writeln (*TTYO*, 'Type one of the following:');
         ...

Alternatively, the mode flags can be a record; each field defines a mode.

mode: **record**
         terse: *boolean*;
         train: *boolean*;
         affix: *boolean*;
         ...
    end;

And reference is then made as,

if *mode.terse*
   then ...
   else ...

The latter form has the advantage of allowing numeric mode settings, since not all options may be easily categorized by a boolean value. The "terseness" of the interaction between the speller and the user may be possible at several levels: level 0 (very terse), level 1 (terse), level 2 (normal), level 3 (verbose), and level 4 (very verbose). This results in code such as,

if *mode.terse* > 2
   then ...

This flexibility might be useful and so we define our mode flags as a record, accessed by *mode.flag*.

9.0   The Main Program

The structure of the main program is easily described by the following.

```
begin
        initialize;
        check_spelling;
        finalize;
end.
```

This is an obvious top level, but indicates an important decomposition. The *initialize* procedure is responsible for the initial user dialog or interpreting the command line for mode settings and file definitions. The *finalize* procedure closes files as necessary and does any other post-processing. Such post-processing may include asking what to do next. In the DEC-10 speller, the following choices are given to the user.

* Quit (return to the time-sharing monitor).

* Create a local dictionary of the words found in this spelling run.

* Circle back to check another file.

* List statistics on the number of tokens checked, the number misspelled, ...

Since it is not unlikely that a user may want to check several files, another possible structure for the main program is:

```
begin
        per_session_initialization;

        repeat
                per_file_initialize;
                check_spelling;
                per_file_conclusion;
        until mode.quit;

        per_session_conclusion;
end.
```

This structure allows multiple files to be corrected but leaves no room for other activities which may be necessary also. These activities may include modifying the dictionary by loading or deleting a local dictionary, setting modes, asking for statistics, and so on. These actions can be allowed in several ways. One speller takes the user through a predefined script, one step at a time as,

```
begin
        initialize;
        repeat
                modify_dictionary;
                set_modes;
                get_input_file;
                get_output_file;
                check_spelling;
                get_end_option;
        until option=quit;
end.
```

The *modify_dictionary* procedure repeatedly asks the user if local dictionaries are to be loaded until the user replies "no"; the *set_modes* procedure lists possible mode settings and asks the user to specify a list of mode settings; and so on. The possible sequences of actions are strictly limited to the sequences defined by the top–level script.

A more flexible system, and the one that we adopt, is to consider the speller as an interpreter — executing the actions specified by the user. With this viewpoint, we define the top level program as,

```
begin
        per_session_initialization;

        repeat
                read_and_obey_speller_directive;
        until mode.quit;

        per_session_conclusion;

end.
```

We distinguish a *session* (which consists of one continuous execution of the spelling program) from checking or correcting a specific file. Several files may be processed in a session.

9.1   *per_session_initialization*

Initialization which is needed for each spelling session consists of,

```
procedure per_session_initialization;
begin
        open_interactive_files;
        initialize_global_variables;
        global_dictionary_initialize;
end;
```

Any or all of these may be null, depending upon our further decisions, and the system in which we implement. For example, much of *initialize_global_variables* can be done by DATA statements in Fortran or the similar construct in assembly language, or it can be done with assignment statements. Thus, initialization can be done at load-time or run-time (or both), as desired.

9.2   *per_session_conclusion*

The end of a session requires little more than

```
procedure per_session_conclusion;
begin
      close_all_remaining_files;
end;
```

which may be a null action if this is automatically done by the operating system upon program termination.

10.0   *read_and_obey_speller_directive*

Central control for the speller is *read_and_obey_speller_directive*. This procedure consists of two parts: first, reading the user command and then executing it. Thus,

```
procedure read_and_obey_speller_directive;
var
      cmd:   command;
begin
      get_command (cmd, table_1);
      execute_table_1_command (cmd);
end;
```

We note several points about this decomposition. First, we have separated the problem of reading the input command (*get_command*) from its execution (*execute_table_1_command*). This allows the input to be in whatever form (numeric or alphabetic) or from whatever source (keyboard, file, or some more exotic input device like a mouse, light pen, voice, or whatever) is desired or possible. Initially, for debugging, we may use a simple numeric read; eventually we want convenient alphabetic input. However it is done, all we are concerned with at this point is that the input command is returned as a *command* type in the parameter *cmd*.

Second, notice that *get_command* is parameterized by a table of commands (*table_1* in this case). This is the result of looking ahead and seeing that there are other circumstances when we will need user input (such as when a misspelled token is found). Also it makes it easier to add new commands; new commands require only the modification of *table_1* and the execution procedure *execute_table_1_command*.

10.1   *execute_table_1_command*

The execution of a particular command is best done by a **case** statement. We choose the following basic structure:

```
procedure execute_table_1_command (cmd: command);
begin

      case cmd of

            help:  list_commands (table_1);

            quit:  mode.quit := true;

            check:  begin
                           mode.correct := false;
                           check_spelling;
                    end;

            correct:  begin
                           mode.correct := true;
                           check_spelling;
                      end;

            clear:  clear_local_dictionary;

            load:  load_local_dictionary;

            dump:  dump_local_dictionary;

            mode:  set_modes;

            statistics:  write_statistics;

      end (* case *);

end;
```

With this code, we have defined the meaning of a command. The available commands are:

help: prints the list of legal commands.

quit: exit program.

check, correct: check or correct a file.

clear, load, dump: manipulate local dictionary files.

mode: set mode switches.

statistics: give useful statistical summaries.

Additional commands can be easily added to the speller by writing the required procedure(s) and adding new lines to the **case** statement and the command table *table_1*.

Before we get into the definition of the procedures used above, let us back up and consider the *get_command* procedure.

11.0 Command Input

Since we are designing an interactive spelling checker, we assume that the input commands come from the user keyboard. Further, we prefer alphabetic keyword commands. A command table is thus a list of alphabetic keywords. These alphabetic keywords are variable–length strings (tokens); a command table is composed of a variable number of these strings. The variable number of entries in a table argues for a linked list representation of the table. Also, if we are going to be using multiple command tables, we need a distinguishing prompt for each. So we define a command table by,

```
command = 0..max_command_table_entries;
command_pool_index = 0..max_command_table_entries;

n_command_pool_entries:  command_pool_index;
command_pool:  array [command_pool_index]
                of record
                        cmd:  command;
                        word:  token_type;
                        next:  command_pool_index;
                end;

command_table = record
                    prompt:  char;
                    next:  command_pool_index;
                end;

table_1:  command_table;
```

A *command_pool_index* is a pointer to a list of command keywords. We define a command pool to hold the command table entries. Each command table entry consists of the alphabetic keyword string (*word*), an associated command (*cmd*), and a pointer to the next command in the table. We could just use the *command_pool_index* as the command number, but use of a separate command field allows several strings to define the same command. Thus *exit* and *quit* can be defined as the same command. We can also extend our list to allow *end* and *stop* to mean the same. Similar synonyms can be allowed for other commands.

Initializing the table defines the keywords, commands and the table to which they should be added.

```
procedure table_1_initialize;
begin
        table_1.prompt := '*';
        table_1.next := null;

        enter_command_table (table_1, help, 'help ');
        enter_command_table (table_1, quit, 'quit ');
        enter_command_table (table_1, quit, 'exit ');
        enter_command_table (table_1, check, 'check ');
        enter_command_table (table_1, correct, 'correct ');
        enter_command_table (table_1, clear, 'clear ');
        enter_command_table (table_1, load, 'load ');
        enter_command_table (table_1, dump, 'dump ');
        enter_command_table (table_1, mode, 'mode ');
        enter_command_table (table_1, statistics, 'statistics ');
end;
```

Now to get a command, we simply read a command string from the user and search the command table. We should consider however that the command may not be found, in which case, we need to read another command. We use the null command to signal that a command was not found.

```
procedure get_command (var cmd: command; table: command_table);
var
        token:  command_word;
begin
        repeat
                read_command (token, table);
                search_command_table (table, token, cmd);
        until cmd ≠ null;
end;
```

To read a command, we first prompt the user, then read each character until an end–of–line. Each character as it is read is converted to lower case to ease searching.

Also we check to be sure that our input buffer is not exceeded. The input command is an array of characters and the length of the array. If a zero–length string is typed, we prompt the user again.

If the user is unsure of the possible inputs, a question mark lists the possible commands and prompts for a new input. This is the same action that a *help* command produces.

```
procedure read_command (var token: command_word; table: command_table);
var
        c:  char;
        j:  token_index;
        question:  boolean;
begin
        repeat

                write (TTYO, table.prompt, ' ');

                j := 0;
                question := false;
                while not eoln (TTYI)
                    do begin
                                read (TTYI, c);
                                if c = '?'
                                    then question := true
                                    else if j < max_token_length
                                            then begin
                                                    j := j + 1;
                                                    token.c[j] := lower_case[c];
                                            end;
                        end;
                    readln (TTYI);

                if question
                    then begin
                                list_commands (table);
                                j := 0;
                        end;

                token.length := j;

        until token.length > 0;
    end;
```

The conversion to lower case is by the array *lower_case* which is defined by,

lower_case: **array** [*char*] **of** *char*;

```
    for c := chr(0) to chr(127)
      do lower_case[c] := c;
    for c := 'A' to 'Z'
      do lower_case[c] := chr( ord(c) − ord('A') + ord('a') );
```

11.1   list_commands

Listing the possible commands is a simple chain following exercise. For each chain entry we print it (*write_token*) and go on to the next chain (*p := p.next*) until we hit the end of the chain (*p = null*).

```
    procedure list_commands (table: command_table);
    var
          p:  command_pool_index;
    begin
          writeln (TTYO);
          writeln (TTYO, 'Commands are:');

          writeln (TTYO, '        ', '? (Help)');

          p := table.next;
          while p ≠ null
            do begin
                      write (TTYO, '      ');
                      write_token (command_pool[p].word);
                      writeln (TTYO);
                      p := command_pool[p].next;
                end;

          writeln (TTYO);
    end;
```

11.2   search_command_table

To search the command table, we can do a simple linear search for equality. However, experience with other interactive programs leads us to believe that users may want to abbreviate their commands as they become more familiar with them. Thus, a command string which is a prefix of a legal command should be taken as specifying the command of which it is a prefix.

To implement this abbreviation capability, we compare the input command with each entry in the command table until an exact match is found. As we search through the table, we keep track of the number of entries of which the command is a prefix. If no exact match is found, but exactly one prefix is found, we assume the input is that command. If the input is a prefix of several commands, the input is ambiguous. If the input is not found or is ambiguous, we return the null command.

```
procedure search_command_table (table: command_table;  token:  command_word;
                                           var cmd:  command);

var
      p:  command_pool_index;
      result:  compare_result;
      n_prefix:  command_pool_index;
      which_prefix:  command_pool_index;
begin
      p := table.next;
      result := less;
      n_prefix := 0;

      while (p ≠ null) and (result ≠ equal)
          do begin

                  compare (token, result, command_pool[p].word);

                  if prefix
                      then begin
                                  n_prefix := n_prefix + 1;
                                  which_prefix := p;
                          end;

                  if result ≠ equal
                      then p := command_pool[p].next;

              end;

      cmd := null;
      if result = equal
          then cmd := command_pool[p].cmd
          else if n_prefix = 0
                  then writeln (TTYO, 'Unknown Command.')
          else if n_prefix = 1
                  then cmd :=command_pool[which_prefix].cmd
          else if n_prefix > 1
                  then writeln (TTYO, 'Ambiguous Command.');

end;
```

12.0   *read_and_obey_speller_directive* (continued)

Now that we can read input commands, let us return to defining the effect of each command. Our previous code was,

```
procedure execute_table_1_command (cmd: command);
begin

    case cmd of

        help:   list_commands (table_1);

        quit:   mode.quit := true;

        check:  begin
                    mode.correct := false;
                    check_spelling;
                end;

        correct: begin
                    mode.correct := true;
                    check_spelling;
                 end;

        clear:  clear_local_dictionary;

        load:   load_local_dictionary;

        dump:   dump_local_dictionary;

        mode:   set_modes;

        statistics:  write_statistics;


    end (* case *);

end;
```

Now we need to define the code for each command.

Some commands are easy to define. The *help* command simply lists the command table (using *list_commands*). The *quit* command (which can be the keyword *quit* or *exit* or *e* or *q* or ...) sets the quit *mode* flag (and causes the outer loop in the main program to stop). We look at the other commands later, but the heart of our program is *check_spelling*, so let us design it next.

13.0   *check_spelling*

Spelling checking or correction is on a file–by–file basis. Thus, for each invocation, we must open and close an input and output file. For each token in the input file, we must search the dictionary for that token, and if it is not found, ask the user if it is correct or not. Our basic flow is thus,

```
procedure check_spelling;
var
        token:   token_type;
        found:   boolean;
begin
        per_file_initialize;

        repeat
                get_token (token);

                search_dictionary (token, found);

                if not found
                    then ask_user_about_it (token);

                output_token (token);

        until mode.end_of_file or mode.quit;

        per_file_conclusion;
end;
```

The initialization and conclusion routines are fairly simple; the major work is in the syntax analysis for token input (*get_token*) and in the dictionary search (*search_dictionary*).

13.1   *per_file_initialize*

For each file to be checked, the following actions are necessary.

```
procedure per_file_initialize;
begin
        get_input_file;
        get_output_file;
        initialize_variables_for_these_files;
        local_dictionary_initialize;
end;
```

The dictionary may need to be initialized for each file to be checked since we may modify the previous (or default) dictionary by local dictionaries between checking files.

The procedure of getting a file name typically involves writing a message to the user, followed by reading a file name specification. The file name is read as a string and then passed to a system routine which interprets the string as a file name and opens the named file, attaching it to the given file identifier, as in,

```
procedure get_input_file;
var
      file_name:  filename;
begin
      write (TTYO, 'Input file name:   ');
      readln (TTYI, file_name);
      reset (INPUT, file_name);
end;

procedure get_output_file;
var
      file_name:  filename;
begin
      write (TTYO, 'Output file name:   ');
      readln (TTYI, file_name);
      rewrite (OUTPUT, file_name);
end;
```

The details of these operations obviously depend greatly on the operating system interface for the particular system being used.

Variables which are specific to these files, such as file buffer pointers, status flags (*mode.end_of_file*, ...), counters, and memory space, need initialization here (*initialize_variables_for_these_files*).

13.2   per_file_conclusion

Finishing up after a file involves only minor clean-up.

```
procedure per_file_conclusion;
begin
      close (INPUT);
      close (OUTPUT);

      writeln (TTYO);
      writeln (TTYO, 'Done.');
end;
```

13.3   check_spelling (continued)

For the bulk of *check_spelling*, two special problems must be considered.

First, the speller must act like a *copy* routine in the case that no spelling changes are made. This means that all characters between tokens must be copied directly from INPUT to OUTPUT. Second, if a suspected spelling error is found, that token must be displayed for the user. We also want to display some of the context surrounding this use of the token. Thus, in general, we want to get not just the next token, but the next token and its context.

These concerns can be brought into the program at this level, by introducing code to handle them, or they can be introduced at lower levels, within the setting of other procedures. We defer consideration of these other concerns until lower level routines. The major impact is in *get_token*.

14.0   get_token

As just mentioned, *get_token* must be carefully written. We actually need to consider not only the next token, but also intermediate non-token characters and keeping the appropriate context for display.

14.1   Display

The display context is a major design problem. We want to display a potentially misspelled token plus sufficient context for its use, and hence its correctness, to be determined. The possible ranges of context include:

* No context (just the token).

* The token and a fixed number of characters before and after.

* The token and the line in which it occurs.

* The token and those characters before it back to the start of the line and forward to the end of the line, but at most *n* characters in either direction (to handle the possible problem of long lines.)

* The line in which the token occurs plus *n* lines before and *n* lines after that line.

Other possibilities exist also. We assume that the display and the input file are sequences of lines. We certainly want to display at least the line in which the token occurs. Also, if possible we would like to show even more context. The constraining factors are communication bandwidth (large context at low speeds requires long waits for display update), and terminal characteristics (a hard copy terminal dictates small context to save paper; a dumb terminal requires substantial retransmission to update a large context on the display; cursor control would be the most reasonable minimum for a CRT). Thus, a general speller, even for use only on one system might need various levels of context. (Much of the code in the DEC–10 speller is concerned with maintaining the display on the wide variety of terminals used.)

To solve this problem we parameterize the amount of context displayed. We assume the input is a set of lines. The display context is composed of three sets of lines, called regions.

An *upper* region (*n_upper* lines)

A *middle* region (*n_middle* lines)

A *lower* region (*n_lower* lines)

The token of concern is always in the middle region somewhere. The lines before the middle region are the upper region and the lines after the middle region are the lower region. The purpose of the upper region is to provide context before the token if it happens to be near the beginning of the middle region; the lower region provides context after the token if it happens to be near the end of the middle region.

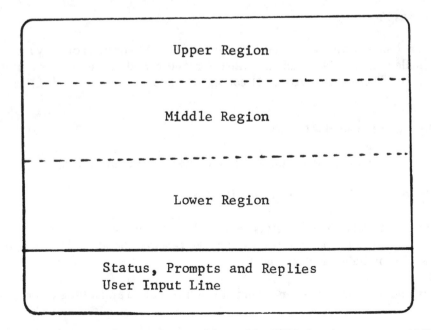

Figure 2. Example layout for a cursor addressable CRT showing upper, middle and
lower context regions.

This definition allows many different possible contexts, depending upon the size of the three regions. If we represent the sizes by the triple (*n_upper*, *n_middle*, *n_lower*), then we can create the following different types of context displays by appropriate selection of the three parameters.

(0, 1, 0) — only the line in which the token occurs.

(1, 1, 1) — the line in which the token occurs and the line before it and after it.

(n, 1, 0) — a block of lines; the token in question is in the last line.

(n, 1, n) — a block of lines; the token in question is in the middle line.

(n, n, n) — if *n* is a third of the number of lines on the screen, then an entire page is displayed. The top third is old context, the spelling checking is going on in the middle third and the bottom third is yet to be checked.

(0, n, 0) — if *n* is the number of lines on a screen, then the token is somewhere on the screen.

The possibilities available encompass most of the schemes which have been proposed for context display. The context defined by (0, 1, 0) is probably the most common. If the suspect token is not always on one easily identified line, then it is best if it is differentiated from all other words by blinking, brightness, reverse video, or some such display property.

The implementation of this scheme requires a buffer of *n_upper+n_middle+n_lower* lines, and appropriate code to manage that buffer. The characters then stream through this buffer as needed. Thus, we isolate the buffer and its management as separate routines, ignoring the buffering and buffer management problems for right now. We assume a procedure *get_character_from_context_buffer* which handles all these problems; this allows us to concentrate on the lexical issues of *get_token*.

14.2   Lexical Issues

The lexical issues of *get_token* revolve around copying characters from INPUT to OUTPUT until we find a token, then isolating that token and returning it. An array of characters, called *token*, is used to return the next token. Its length is also handy and is returned in *token.length*.

```
token_length = 0..max_token_length;
token_index  = 0..max_token_length;
```

```
token_type = record
                length:  token_length;
                c:    array [token_index] of char;
          end;
```

Now what is a token? Certainly any sequence of alphabetic characters surrounded by delimiters. The upper and lower case alphabetic characters are alphabetic while most special characters (like period, comma, and so on) are delimiters. Several special cases arise, including numbers, hyphens and apostrophes.

Numbers are not normally considered tokens. How can we determine that "10" is or is not correctly spelled? Combinations of letters and numbers like "IBM360" may be or may not be tokens; we had best leave this as a mode option, *mode.mixed_alphanumerics*. For good measure, let us also define an option, *mode.number_check* which indicates that we should check numbers. Since these numbers will not be in the dictionary, we will ask the user about each one, as they are found.

Hyphens generally combine two tokens into a compound word. Since the individual tokens must be correctly spelled, we can treat hyphens as delimiters. One other use is to separate a word across line boundaries when the entire word does not fit on one line. Text justification and formatting programs have generally eliminated the need to consider such things in the documents stored on-line, and so we do not consider this use of the hyphen here. Another option could be defined which worries about hyphens at the ends of lines.

(I think everyone realizes however that hyphenation is not computably reversible. Consider splitting "grandmother" between two lines, yielding the sequence "grand-|mother". The hyphen is removed and the two tokens "grand" and "mother" are combined into one word. However, if "great-grandmother" is hyphenated in this situation, we have the sequence "great-|grandmother". Here we do not delete the hyphen. Thus, end-of-line hyphenation cannot in general be undone.)

Apostrophes must certainly be considered parts of tokens when used inside a token, such as in contractions. However, some people use them as quote symbols also. But, since apostrophes can occur at the end of possessive forms and at the beginning of some dialects, we cannot determine when they are used for these purposes instead of quotes. Consider <'Twas the Jones' car>. We therefore treat apostrophes like letters when they are adjacent to tokens — an isolated apostrophe is treated as a delimiter. Further, we might consider a token with both leading and trailing apostrophes as a misuse of apostrophes as quotes and strip them off. However, this would be rare and there is no harm in asking the user about a few more rare cases, so we do not program that feature now.

Our analysis leads to three or four classes of characters:

character_class = (alphabetic, numeric, delimiter, apostrophe);

We could simply label an apostrophe as an alphabetic character and reduce the number of classes to three, but it seems unnecessary. We scan characters until we get a non–delimiter, then we have a sequence of non–delimiters. This sequence can be:

pure alphabetic — a token.

pure numeric — a token only if *mode.number_check* is true.

pure apostrophes — not a token.

alphabetic and numeric — a token only if *mode.mixed_alphanumerics* is true.

alphabetic and apostrophes — a token.

numeric and apostrophes — a token only if *mode.number_check* is true or maybe only if *mode.mixed_alphanumerics* is true, or maybe not a token?

alphabetic, numeric, and apostrophes — a token if *mode.mixed_alphanumerics* is true.

Other cases include:

Too long a sequence — not a token.

Strictly upper case alphabetics — a token unless *mode.ignore_upper_case* is true.

The class of a character and its upper case or lower case attribute are best defined by constant arrays indexed by a character.

```
class:  array [char] of character_class;
upper_or_lower:  array [char] of (upper, lower, neither);

for i := chr(0) to chr(127) do class[i] := delimiter;
for i := '0' to '9' do class[i] := numeric;
for i := 'A' to 'Z' do class[i] := alphabetic;
for i := 'a' to 'z' do class[i] := alphabetic;
class[''''] := apostrophe;

for i := chr(0) to chr(127) do upper_or_lower[i] := neither;
for i := 'A' to 'Z' do upper_or_lower[i] := upper;
for i := 'a' to 'z' do upper_or_lower[i] := lower;
```

The token, or non-token nature of a potential token sequence of characters can be defined by a set over the character class (alphabetic, numeric, apostrophe) indicating whether the given class of character is or is not in the sequence. The code copies delimiters until a nondelimiter is found, then saves characters until another delimiter is found (or the sequence is too long), keeping track of the set of character classes encountered. Then a decision is made on the "tokenness" of the sequence. If it is not a token, we output it and loop back to continue this process until a token is finally found (or end-of-file).

```
procedure get_token (var token: token_type);
var
        c:  char;
        is_token:  boolean;
begin

        get_character_from_context_buffer (c);

    repeat
            find_non_delimiter (c);

            if c = end_of_file
                then begin
                            mode.end_of_file := true;
                            token.length := 0;
                    end
                else begin
                            collect_possible_token (c, token);
                            determine_if_token (is_token, token);
                            if not is_token
                                then copy_to_delimiter (token, c);
                    end;

        until is_token or mode.end_of_file;

        put_character_back_in_context_buffer (c);
end;
```

Notice that, as is usual for lexical analysis, we must look one character ahead to determine the end of a token. Thus, we must put that character back when we find that we have gone too far and are at the end of a token.

To find a non-delimiter, we simply,

```
procedure find_non_delimiter (var c: char);
begin
        while (class[c] = delimiter) and (c ≠ end_of_file)
            do begin   (* skip delimiters *)
                    put_output (c);
```

```
                       get_character_from_context_buffer (c);
            end;
  end;
```

To collect a sequence of non–delimiter characters as a possible token,

```
procedure collect_possible_token (var c: char; var token: token_type);
begin
        token.length := 0;
        while (class[c] ≠ delimiter) and (token.length < max_token_length)
            do begin
                    token.length := token.length + 1;
                    token.c[token.length] := c;
                    get_character_from_context_buffer (c);
            end;

        (* end of collection; delimiter or too long *)
end;
```

Once we have collected a sequence of characters, we must determine if we have
a token. Three cases must be considered: (1) the sequence was too long; (2) the sequence contains numeric digits or apostrophes; and (3) the sequence is entirely upper
case. This leads to:

```
procedure determine_if_token (var is_token: boolean; token: token_type);
begin
        if token.length ≥ max_token_length
            then is_token := false (* too long *)
            else begin
                    check_class_of_token (is_token, token);
                    if is_token
                        then check_all_uppers (is_token, token);
            end;
end;
```

To check the type of token collected, we compute the set of character–classes in
the token. This set is used in a case statement to decide if the collection is a token.

```
procedure check_class_of_token (var is_token: boolean; token: token_type);
var
        cc:  character_class;
        class_set:  set of character_class;

        i:  token_index;
```

```
begin
        class_set := [];
        class_type := 0;

        for i := 1 to token.length
        do class_set := class_set + [class[token.c[i]]];

        (* * * * * * * * * * * * * * * * * * * * * * * *)

        case class_set of

          [ alphabetic ]:
                            is_token := true;

          [ numeric ]:
                            is_token := mode.number_check;

          [ alphabetic, numeric ]:
                            is_token := mode.mixed_alphanumerics;

          [ apostrophe ]:
                            is_token := false;

          [ alphabetic, apostrophe ]:
                            is_token := true;

          [ numeric, apostrophe ]:
                            is_token := mode.number_check
                                       and mode.mixed_alphanumerics;

          [ alphabetic, numeric, apostrophe ]:
                            is_token := mode.mixed_alphanumerics;

        end (* case *);

    end;
```

Finally, if we have been told to ignore strictly upper case tokens, we need to check that at least one character is lower case. (This implies that apostrophes and digits are considered upper case.)

```
procedure check_all_uppers (var is_token: boolean; token: token_type);
var
        i:   token_index;
begin
        if mode.ignore_uppers
          then begin
```

```
                    i := token.length;
                    while (i > 0) and (upper_or_lower[token.c[i]] ≠ lower)
                        do i := i - 1;
                    is_token := (i = 0);
            end;
    end;
```

If we do find that we have collected a non-token, then we must copy it to the
output file and skip over any remaining non–delimiter characters (in case the token
was too long).

```
    procedure copy_to_delimiter (token: token_type; var c: char);
    var
            i:  token_index;
    begin
            (* output token buffer *)
            for i := 1 to token.length
             do put_output (token.c[i]);

            (* now if token was too long copy to next delimiter *)
            while class[c] ≠ delimiter
                do begin
                        put_output (c);
                        get_character_from_context_buffer (c);
                    end;
    end;
```

14.3   Display (revisited)

The context buffer routines must manage the maintenance of the information
which is needed to provide context for identifying suspicious tokens. Since we im-
agine the display to be a line oriented terminal (printing or CRT), we define the context buffer to be an array of lines. Each line is an array of characters which define one
display line. The lines are divided into three regions: upper, middle, and lower, as
defined earlier, by the three parameters, n_upper, n_middle, and n_lower. These
variables are the number of lines in each region. Thus the total number of lines which
must be managed is

```
    n_lines = n_upper + n_middle + n_lower;

    begin_upper = 1;
    end_upper = n_upper;
```

begin_middle = *end_upper*+1;
end_middle = *begin_lower*+*n_middle*−1;

begin_lower = *end_middle*+1;
end_lower = *begin_lower*+*n_lower*−1;

Two separate constraints dictate the content of the context buffer. First, each character which is read must be output exactly the same; *no* changes are allowed (to correct "nonstandard" file forms, for example). We must store and pass on exactly and only the characters read.

Second, we want the internal line structure to reflect the actual view presented on the screen. Thus, short lines are stored as short lines. Long lines should be automatically wrapped around to the next line, so that a single input line may occupy several lines of the context buffer.

Another problem is the treatment of non-printing characters (control characters). Many of these characters can cause cursor motion or other changes in the display (such as clearing the screen). Since the speller should be in complete control of the display, we must prevent such actions, while still displaying what the actual input characters are. The traditional solution is to represent control characters by two characters. Thus, a control-G is represented by the sequence "^G". We use that approach.

This means, however, that not all characters are only one display position wide. On a line length of 80 characters, 80 "G" characters can be displayed, but only 40 control-G characters can be displayed. To accommodate this difference, we define a constant array of strings, indexed by a character, for the display representation of the character and its length.

```
display_form:   array [char]
                  of record
                             length:  0..2;
                             representation:  array [1..2] of char;
                  end;

for i := chr(0) to chr(31) do with display_form[i]
  do begin
        length := 2;
        representation[1] := '^';
        representation[2] := chr(ord(i)+64);
    end;
for i := chr(32) to chr(126) do with display_form[i]
  do begin
        length := 1;
        representation[1] := i;
    end;
```

```
for i := chr(127) to chr(127) do with display_form[i]
  do begin
        length := 2;
        representation[1] := '^';
        representation[2] := '_';
     end;
```

The context buffer management routines are parameterized by several constants. The sizes of the three regions define the number of lines needed. The length of a line (*line_length*) is defined by the line length of the display terminal. We need enough room in each line for *line_length* characters plus additional room for an end-of-line character.

```
line_index = 0..line_length+1;

line = record
            length:  line_index;
            c:  array [line_index] of char;
        end;

line_number = 0..max_lines;

context_buffer:  array [line_number] of line;

current_position:  record
                        line:  line_number;
                        column:  line_index;
                    end;
```

Now to get a character from the buffer, we simply update the current position pointer and get the next character.

```
procedure get_character_from_context_buffer (var c: char);
begin
        update_current_position;
        with current_position
          do c := context_buffer[line].c[column];
end;
```

The *update_current_position* procedure normally just adds one to the current character position; advancing to the next character. This allows the procedure *put_character_back_in_context_buffer* to simply subtract one. In both cases we must worry about line changes. Since we know that we only put, at most, one character back in the buffer (between calls to get it back), we can ignore the possible problems with trying to back up too far or at the wrong times.

```
procedure put_character_back_in_context_buffer (c: char);
begin
      with current_position
         do column := column - 1;
end;
```

However, in moving forward, we need to consider the action necessary when we move to the next line. Moving to the next line may move us out of the middle region into the lower region. If this is true, then we must adjust our regions, moving the middle region into the upper, the lower to the middle and new input into the lower region.

```
procedure update_current_position;
begin
         with current_position
            do begin
                     if column < context_buffer[line].length
                        then column := column + 1
                        else repeat
                                   column := 1;

                                   if line < end_middle
                                      then line := line + 1
                                      else begin
                                                  reset_regions;
                                                  line := begin_middle;
                                           end;
                                   until column ≤ context_buffer[line].length;
               end;
end;
```

14.4   reset_regions

The code for adjusting regions when we are finished with the current middle region must consider that the three regions need not be of equal size, or even of non--zero size. The upper and lower regions should just float along around the middle region however, so the new definition of the middle region dictates the necessary changes for the other two regions. A little thought and computation shows that the entire context buffer is shifted up *n_middle* lines. The top *n_middle* lines are discarded, and *n_middle* new lines must be read in to fill the bottom *n_middle* lines. Thus the code to adjust the regions is:

```
procedure reset_regions;
var
      i: line_number;
```

```
    begin
            for i := 0 to n_lines-n_middle
              do context_buffer[i] := context_buffer[i+n_middle];
            for i := n_lines-n_middle+1 to n_lines
              do read_line (i);
    end;
```

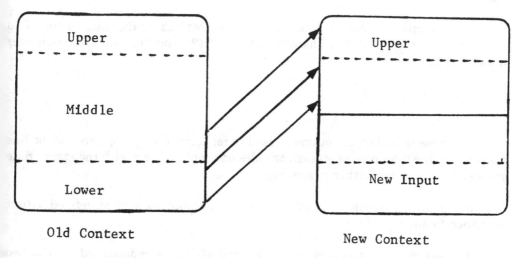

Figure 3. The change in context in *reset_regions* moves all lines in the old context up
          n_middle_lines, reading new lines as necessary.

14.5   *Character Set Concerns*

At this point it becomes difficult to continue ignoring how the end-of-line condition is represented. In general we are assuming that our character set is ASCII
(although the change to other character sets such as EBCDIC is trivial). We are
reading and writing the INPUT and OUTPUT files by characters. This is functional-
ly what is needed.

The major problem is the representation of the end-of-line condition. ASCII
has two characters which relate to end-of-line: CR (carriage return) and LF (line
feed). Conventionally a CR/LF pair defines an end-of-line. However, some systems
use only a CR (e.g., Data General Nova systems), others only a LF (e.g., UNIX) and
still other systems use other characters (such as the unit separator character). We
want to avoid either limiting our program to working only on one of these systems or
having to explicitly program for all of these conditions. Thus, we need to abstract the
representation of the end-of-line marker from the ASCII representation.

One technique that has been useful on a wide variety of systems, is to define a new, expanded character set more closely reflecting the semantics of the assumed input. New characters are called *pseudo–characters*, and represent the information that is needed, independent of the form of its input. The input characters are represented by their ordinal values, as small integers. The type of these items is *pseudo_char*, a user-defined subrange. This allows the definition of new characters which are created and interpreted by the program, but are not in the standard character set.

For example, the ASCII character set is represented by the integers from 0 to 127. We assign the end–of–line character a value of 128, and the end–of–file character a value of 129.

   pseudo_char = 0..129;

A simple lexical input routine is used to recognize the appropriate end–of–line and end–of–file sequences or status variables and replace them with the appropriate pseudo–character for further processing.

On output, a pseudo–character causes the appropriate system defined output sequence to appear.

For example, in a system where an end–of–line is represented by the two character sequence CR/LF, we replace each CR/LF sequence by an end–of–line pseudo–character on input, and replace each end–of–line pseudo–character with the sequence CR/LF on output.

We must revise all the existing design to replace the use of the *char* type with the *pseudo_char* type.

14.6   read_line

Now to read a line, we read characters one at a time until an end–of–line condition occurs (and the end–of–line character is in the context buffer), or until the line is full.

```
procedure read_line (i: line_number);
var
        j:  line_index;
        display_length:  line_index;
        c:  char;
begin
        j := 0  (* number of characters read into line *);
        display_length := 0;
```

```
      repeat
            j := j + 1;
            read (INPUT, c);
            display_length := display_length + display_form[c].length;
            context_buffer[i].c[j] := c;

      until (c = end_of_line) or (c = end_of_file)
         or (display_length ≥ line_length);

         context_buffer[i].length := j;
   end;
```

A couple of interesting problems arise here when we reach boundary conditions. First, notice that *display_length* need not increase by one all the time; it may increase by 2 in the case of a control character. So suppose the line length is 80, we have 79 positions filled, room for one more display character on this line, and the next character is a control character. It won't fit, so we have to put it back.

We may have to put characters back in the input. Thus, we need to replace our *read*s with a *get_char_from_buffer*, and provide one more layer of buffering between the program and the input file. The more complex *read_line* procedure is then,

```
procedure read_line (i: line_number);
var
      c:  pseudo_char;
      j:  line_index;
      display_length:  0..line_length+2;
begin
      j := 0;
      display_length := 0;

      repeat
            j := j + 1;
            get_char_from_input (c);
            display_length := display_length + display_form[c].length;
            context_buffer[i].c[j] := c;

      until (c=end_of_line) or (c=end_of_file)
         or (display_length > line_length);

      while display_length > line_length
         do begin
                  c := context_buffer[i].c[j];
                  put_char_back_in_input (c);
                  display_length := display_length - display_form[c].length;
                  j := j - 1;
            end;
```

```
        context_buffer[i].length := j;

   end;
```

14.6.1   get_char_from_input and put_char_back_in_input

These routines serve two purposes. They act as buffers for our one–character look–ahead in the context buffer manager. They also convert from the *char* form of character representation to our *pseudo_char* form.

We need a flag *character_saved* to indicate if a character has been put back by the context buffer manager, and the character *saved_character*. If no character has been saved, we read from the actual input file.

```
procedure get_char_from_input (var c: pseudo_char);
begin
      if character_saved
         then begin
                  c := saved_character;
                  character_saved := false;
              end
         else get_input (c);
end;



procedure put_char_back_in_input (c: char);
begin
      character_saved := true;
      saved_character := c;
end;
```

For purposes of modularity, we separate out the translation from *char* to *pseudo_char* representation in a *get_input* procedure. In the code below, we assume that an end–of–line is represented by a CR/LF sequence.

```
procedure get_input (var c: pseudo_char);
const
      CR = 13;
      LF = 10;
var
      cc:  char;
begin
      if eof (INPUT)
         then c := end_of_file
         else begin
                  read (INPUT, cc);
```

```
if (ord(cc) ≠ CR) or (ord(INPUT˄) ≠ LF)
   then c := ord(cc)
   else begin
              c := end_of_line;
              read (INPUT, cc);
         end;
   end;
end;
```

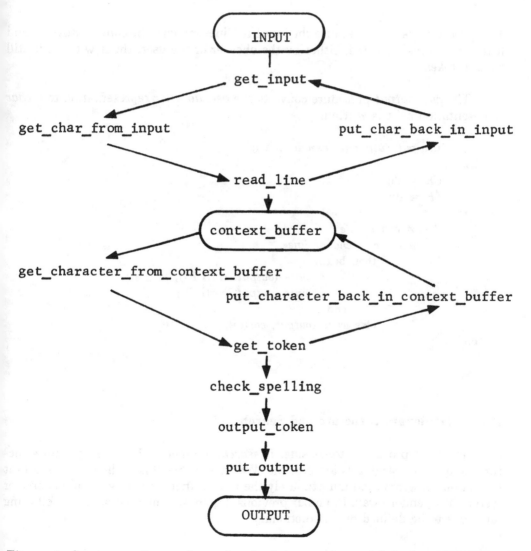

Figure 4. Sequence of procedures involved in copying a token from INPUT to OUTPUT.

14.7   output_token

Closely related to *get_token* is of course *output_token*. We have designed our input so that this is quite easy. Basically, it is,

```
procedure output_token (token: token_type);
var
      j:  token_index;
begin
      for j := 1 to token.length
        do put_output (token.c[j]);
end;
```

This procedure is easier because the input routines manage the context display, and if the token was corrected, either by the checker or the user, the new token is still kept in *token*.

The *put_output* procedure converts the *pseudo_char* representation to a *char* representation as it is written.

```
procedure put_output (c: pseudo_char);
const
      CR = 13;
      LF = 10;
begin
      if c ≠ end_of_file
        then if c = end_of_line
              then begin
                            write (output, chr(CR));
                            write (output, chr(LF));
                    end
              else write (output, chr(c));
end;
```

15.0   Dictionary Structure and Search

The next procedure to consider is *search_dictionary*. Here many data structures and search strategies are possible. We expect that this is the most important part of our program, and unfortunately the most difficult to design in a machine or system independent way. From our previous design, we know we have the following functions to be defined on the dictionary.

1. Search the dictionary for *token* which has *token.length* characters (*search_dictionary*).

2. Add the tokens from the local dictionary on the external file LOCAL to the disk dictionary (*load_local_dictionary*).

3. Create a new local dictionary on the external file LOCAL from the tokens which have been added to the dictionary so far (*dump_local_dictionary*).

4. Reset the dictionary to its initial state before any modifications by local dictionaries (*clear_local_dictionary*).

Looking ahead to our spelling correction task, we may also have,

5. Add *token* to the dictionary.

6. Remember *token* as a misspelling and the correct spelling *new_token*.

This last requirement may be more reasonably handled by an in-core symbol table. Requirement 5 should be similar to requirement 2.

Several factors influence our choice of data structures.

1. The amount of core memory available.

2. The size of the master dictionary.

3. The amount of secondary storage available.

4. The types of secondary storage (fixed disks, floppy disk, the number of drives, the number of simultaneously open files, and so on) and the type of access allowed (direct or sequential).

5. Physical versus virtual memory. A virtual memory means we must carefully design our algorithm to avoid page faults.

6. The processor instruction set for comparing tokens. (Is there a compare n bytes memory to memory or only a register to memory compare instruction? How many characters per word? The IBM 370 can compare entire strings with one instruction; the DEC-10 can compare up to 5 characters using a packed representation of 5 characters per word. The PDP-11 can compare one or two characters using byte or word mode, register or memory to register or memory. Most microprocessors can only compare character by character.

7. The expected search statistics.

The major problem is with the management of local dictionaries. Two approaches seem reasonable.

1. If sufficient memory is available, then all dictionaries can be stored in one large merged in-core dictionary. Each word is tagged as to whether it is in a local dictionary or not. The in-core data structure (hash table, tree, or whatever) needs to support both additions and deletions.

2. If sufficient memory is not available, files are used to support the dictionary. In this case, each local dictionary is kept as a separate file. One special file represents the current dictionary. This file is produced from the master dictionary by adding and deleting local dictionaries as directed by the user. All searches are to this one file. If a single token is to be added to the dictionary, then it is added to this file and simultaneously to the end of the file for the appropriate local dictionary. All files need to be sorted when used. One advantage of this approach is that creating a new local file simply requires renaming or copying the existing local dictionary file.

   This approach really needs direct access to the dictionary. Such an approach allows an in-core index to the dictionary file to be created when the file is produced. By keeping the dictionary sorted, a search of the dictionary requires a binary search of the index, reading in only the one appropriate block and a search of that one block. By keeping several blocks in memory and replacing them on an LRU basis, the number of disk reads might be further reduced.

The first approach, using an in-core dictionary, requires a very large (virtual) memory, but given that, the design problems are reasonable. A hash table such as used by the DEC-10 speller is quite adequate.

However, most systems probably do not have this large memory. Thus, we design our system to use disk files. We assume the ability to represent several thousand bytes in memory, and to maintain multiple external files, as necessary. Further, we assume a direct access file capability. We are designing for a system composed of a minicomputer or micro-processor system with on-line disk storage and 16K to 64K bytes of memory.

It is very important to note that if the dictionary structure should need to be changed, only this one module of our speller needs to be changed — none of our other design work depends upon the actual dictionary structure. This is especially desirable because the two major factors in deciding on an appropriate data structure (memory size and usage statistics) are subject to change from machine to machine and environment to environment.

The usage statistics of the words in the dictionary have the most influence upon our data structure. For example, if we assume that all words are equally likely to be referenced, the appropriate data structure is a large, one-level data structure. However, our belief is that the number of unique words in a document, even a very large document, is relatively small (most authors have only a small active vocabulary), and further, that word usage statistics are very skewed — a small number of words account for a large proportion of actual tokens. These two observations lead us to a three-level dictionary structure. The three dictionaries are:

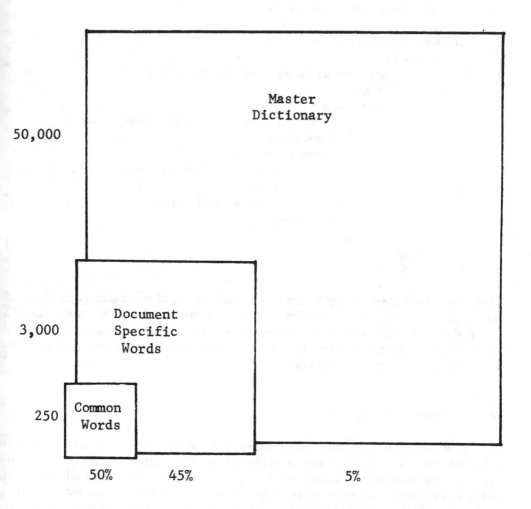

Figure 5. A model of the use and number of words in English text. The three collections of words vary in size (vertical label) and usage (horizontal label).

1. small, in-core dictionary of common English words.

2. words used in this document.

3. entire dictionary.

The *search_dictionary* routine is then,

```
procedure search_dictionary (token: token_type; var found: boolean);
var
      search_token:  search_token_type;
begin
  found := false;
  translate_for_search (token, search_token);

  if search_token.length > 0
      then begin
              search_common_words (search_token, found);
              if not found
                then begin
                        search_document_words (search_token, found);
                        if not found
                          then begin
                                  search_disk_dictionary (search_token, found);
                                  if found
                                      then add_to_list_of_document_words (token)
                              end;
                     end;
           end;
  end;
```

This structure is used mainly to limit both the amount of main storage needed and the number of disk accesses needed. However, it can still be useful in a system in which all dictionaries are kept in memory since we expect the size and search times of these three dictionaries to increase from the list of common words to the list of document words to the disk dictionary.

15.1   *translate_for_search*

One further note before we examine each of our sub-dictionaries. On input our *token* can be any arbitrary sequence of characters. We want to modify the representation of this token for the search. At the minimum we want to reduce all characters to the same case (upper or lower; we choose lower). Also, delimiters are not allowed in the token. This means that we are searching for a very limited character set, only lower case letters and (possibly) numbers.

We can save space by using a limited character set. The dictionary-search-character-set consists of:

(0) A null character.
(1-26) Lower case letters.
(27) Apostrophe
(28-37) Numeric digits.

Unfortunately, there are more than 32 of these restricted characters, so we cannot use a five-bit representation. (If we could justify not storing numeric tokens, or tokens with mixed alphabetic and numeric characters, we could reduce our representation to five bits per character.) However, 6 bits is quite sufficient and it would be possible to use a radix-40 representation for packed strings, if desired. (Radix-40 packs 3 characters into one 16-bit word by noting that if a, b, c are less than 40, then $((a*40)+b)*40+c$ is less than $40*40*40 = 64,000$ which is less than 65, 536 which is 16-bits.)

> *search_char* = 0..39;

Using this new character set, we translate the token into a new representation in *search_token*. If any character in the token is not one of those in the restricted character set, we need not search. All the words in the dictionary are known to use only characters from the restricted set. Rejects are signalled by *search_token.length* = 0.

```
procedure translate_for_search (token: token_type;
                                var search_token:  search_token_type);
    var
        i:  token_index;
        reject:  boolean;
    begin
        reject := false;
        i := token.length;

        while (i > 0) and not reject
            do begin
                    search_token.c[i] := search_code[token.c[i]];
                    if search_token.c[i] = 0
                        then reject := true;
                    i := i - 1;
            end;

        if reject
            then search_token.length := 0
            else search_token.length := token.length;
    end;
```

search_code: **array** [*pseudo_char*] **of** *search_char*;

for *i* := 0 **to**   130 **do** *search_code*[*i*] := 0;
for *i* := *ord*('a') **to** *ord*('z') **do** *search_code*[*i*] := *i* − *ord*('a') + 1;
for *i* := *ord*('A') **to** *ord*('Z') **do** *search_code*[*i*] := *i* − *ord*('A') + 1;
search_code[*ord*('''')] := 27;
for *i* := *ord*('0') **to** *ord*('9') **do** *search_code*[*i*] := *i* − *ord*('0') + 28;

Now let us look at the structure of each of our dictionaries.

15.2   The List of Common Words

From the Brown Corpus [Kucera and Francis 1967], and other studies, we know that about 100 to 200 words account for over half the tokens used in normal English. Thus, a table of these words requires only a relatively small amount of memory, but results in finding a large number of tokens. This table is a static data structure, so we can select a data structure to optimize its search.

The table can either be built at compile time, in a DATA statement form, or during initialization by reading from a standard file. This latter approach allows somewhat more flexibility, since it allows the words to be varied if statistics gathered during use of the speller indicate this is appropriate. However, this is a concern mainly of the initialization routine, so we ignore it for the moment.

Several search strategies are possible. We can sort the list and use a binary search. This has the advantage of a fast search and approximately the same time for all misses. The time to decide that a token is not in the list (a miss) is important since as many as half the searches may be misses. A frequency weighted tree search is somewhat better for those tokens in the tree, but might be worse for those not in the tree. Similarly with the median split search tree strategy. We want to quickly determine that a token is not a common word.

A further problem with these search strategies is that they require comparing *strings* at a time. This may not be easily done on all machines. Particularly looking at minicomputer and microprocessor based systems, we prefer a system which compares only a character at a time. The trie approach is fast, but requires more space than we want to use, so we modify the basic trie structure.

Our basic data structure is a tree. At the root of the tree, we have a branch for each possible initial letter of a token. These branches are to new subtrees where the next letter is used to branch again and so on. For example, for the set of words: "there", "that", and "for", we have:

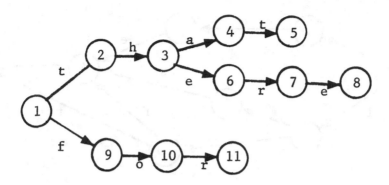

Now to recognize "that", we start at node 1. From 1 under a "t" we go to 2, then we go to 3 under the "h", then to 4 under the "a", and then to 5 under the "t". Now we are at a leaf of the tree and the end of the word, so we accept the token. For the token "thet", we go from 1 to 2 to 3 to 6, and then find that "t" cannot follow "the", so the token is rejected.

The tree above happens to be a binary tree, but in general the number of branches from a node depends upon the number of letters which may follow the prefix recognized so far. Each node can be thought of as a list of pairs — each pair is a letter and the new node to go to under that letter.

Notice that this data structure can save a fair amount of space. All common prefixes of words are automatically collapsed to reduce space. Similar collapsing can be done with common suffixes, as in the following tree for "last", "left", "let", and "feet". The original tree is:

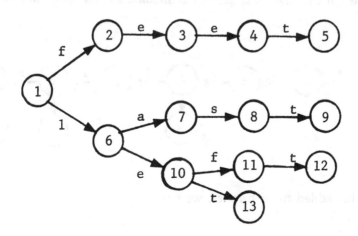

But notice that the four "t" branches are identical, and so we can replace the above tree with the following graph:

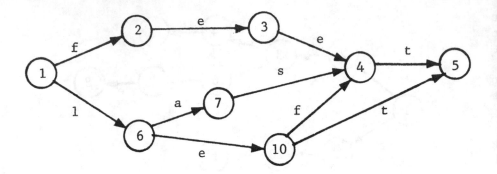

Notice that we cannot collapse the "-et" from "feet" with the "-et" from "let" because of the word "left", but nonetheless, we reduced the number of nodes from 13 to 8.

   Another consideration is how to recognize the ends of words. Consider the set of words, "the", "their", and "theirs". The graph is

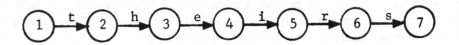

but somehow we must indicate that this is a three-word graph, not simply the one word "theirs". Two approaches are possible: (1) we can add a special "letter" to the end of each word to signal end-of-word, or (2) we can tag nodes as legitimate end-of-words. In the first case, using a semicolon as an end-of-word delimiter, we have,

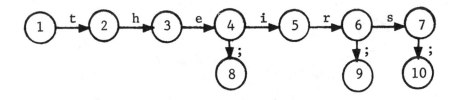

With a tag bit added to each letter, we have,

using an apostrophe to indicate the ends of words. Note that the delimiter approach requires one more entry on the list of successor nodes for each word and although these can be right collapsed, at least the extra pointer is needed. So slightly more space and search time might be needed. Using ASCII character code in an 8–bit byte machine, we expect to be able to squeeze one extra bit out of each character fairly easily, so we use a special bit to indicate end–of–word.

Our next problem is how to represent the list of successors at each node. Again two representations seem reasonable: (1) a linked list and (2) a contiguous list with a length indication. Remember that for the duration of the speller, the entire data structure is static and so we need not consider the ease or difficulty of constructing the data structure, only of its use.

Using the contiguous list approach, we have a node representation of

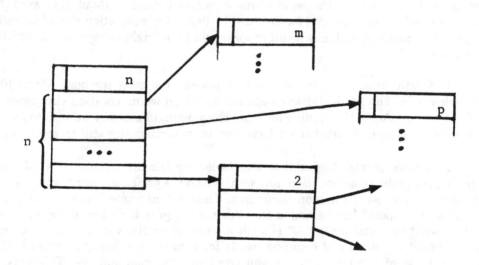

where each list element has a character, end–of–word bit, and a next node pointer.

The linked list representation requires a list of nodes each of which is of the form:

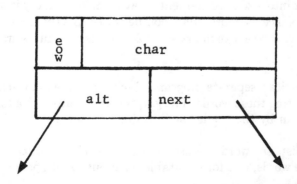

Each node has a character, end–of–word bit, a next pointer and an alternative pointer which points to the remaining list of alternative pointers for this node.

Search times should be roughly the same for either representation. In terms of space, we need at least 5 bits per character, one bit for end–of–word, and maybe 10 to 12 bits per pointer. Tests with the most common 250 words indicate about 1100 unique characters, but only about 450 lists, and each of these lists has an average of only 1 or 2 elements. Out of the 450 lists, 365 have only 1 element, 43 have two, about 15 have 3 or 4, 8 have 5 and only one or two have more than five elements in the list. The first one, for example, has 23 since most letters are possible as first letters. (Remember this is only the most common 250 words, so no "q", "x", "z" or such words.)

With careful packing, the linked representation takes only 2 16–bit words (4 bytes) per link–node, while the contiguous representation requires 2, 3, or more words per node. Total space for the set of words mentioned above is about 1114 words for contiguous allocation and 1324 for linked. The linked representation should be easier to program, however, and may result in some additional right collapse opportunities, so we use it.

The data structure is initialized to represent the most frequent 100 to 1000 English words. The particular size depends on which words are used (frequency of use may depend upon the application) and the amount of memory we wish to use for this data structure. Remember we have two more dictionaries still to represent.

Two more points. Notice that after selecting the most common words, and building the graph representation, any word which is a prefix of a word in the list can be added to the list of common words free. Thus if "important" is on the list, then "imp" and "import" can be added free. All they require is setting the appropriate end–of–word bit. Also since "–s" is such a common suffix, we can add all correct words which are plurals of common words for a minor overhead. Remember that right–collapse of the tree into a graph combines common suffixes. This may be desirable or not, since although the added words may occur infrequently, the cost of adding them is small.

Finally, to speed the initial search, we use an array indexed by character to get started. This reduces the initial step from a search of the 23 possible first letter nodes to simply an index into a 26 or so element array. If more memory is needed, the small amount of extra space is more than compensated by the reduced search time. However, in fact, we can save memory since 23 alternate pointers are not needed with this approach.

We need to write a separate program which reads a list of words and constructs the graph representing those words. The graph is then output in a form which can be conveniently read in by the speller at initialization time.

Appendix I lists the words we use; Appendix II is a list of the nodes for a graph representing these words, in a form suitable for input to the speller during initialization.

Our definition of our graph of linked list elements is:

node_index = 0..*max_number_of_nodes*;

node = **record**
          c: *search_char*;
          end_of_word: *boolean*;
          next: *node_index*;
          alt: *node_index*;
      end;

graph: **array** [*node_index*] **of** *node*;

The first 26 entries of the graph are the entry points into the graph for words starting with the corresponding character ("a" is 1, "b" is 2, ...).

The basic approach to searching the graph is to index with the first character. Then, using the next character, search the *.alt* list. If the next character is found, then we continue with the *.next* node; otherwise, the token is not in the graph. When we get to the end of the token, check the end–of–word bit. The code is,

```
procedure search_common_words (search_token: search_token_type;
                               var found:  boolean);
var
      j:  token_index;
      p:  node_index;
begin
      j := 1; (* steps from 1 to search_token.length *)
      p := search_token.c[j]; (* pointer into node in graph *)

      while (j < search_token.length) and (p ≠ null)
         do begin
                 j := j + 1;
                 p := graph[p].next;
                 while (p ≠ null) and (graph[p].c < search_token.c[j])
                    do p := graph[p].alt;
                 if graph[p].c ≠ search_token.c[j]
                    then p := null;
            end;

      found := (p ≠ null) and graph[p].end_of_word;
end;
```

(Note that either the **and** operations must be optimized so that if *p* = *null*, the right operand is not evaluated, a conditional **and**, or we need to initialize *graph*[0] to be defined, but not used.)

The small amount of code needed for this procedure is a good reflection on our data structure; only two simple loops are needed to search the list of common words. Also, we expect over fifty percent of all tokens to be found in this search. (Tests show that this expectation is correct, at least for my writing style.)

The only point we haven't really mentioned is that the lists of alternative characters at each node are kept sorted — this allows the inner loop to use a less-than comparison, resulting in a slightly faster search in the failure cases.

The initialization of the graph by reading from a file 'COMMON.GPH' in the form of Appendix II is,

```
procedure initialize_common_words_graph;
var
      i:   node_index;
      c:   char;
      skip:  char; (* for skipping over formatting characters *)
begin
      for i := 0 to max_number_of_nodes
        do with graph[i]
            do begin
                      c := null;
                      end_of_word := false;
                      next := null;
                      alt := null;
                end;

      reset (INPUT, 'COMMON.GPH');

      readln (INPUT, i) (* number of links *);

      while not eof (INPUT)
        do begin
                  read (INPUT, i);
                  read (INPUT, skip); (* : *)
                  read (INPUT, skip); (* [ *)
                  read (INPUT, c);

                  if i=0 (* index with character *)
                      then i := search_code[ord(c)];
                  graph[i].c := search_code[ord(c)];

                  read (INPUT, c);
                  if c = '''' (* end of word flag *)
                      then graph[i].end_of_word := true;

                  read (INPUT, skip); (* , *)
                  read (INPUT, graph[i].next);
```

```
              read (INPUT, skip); (* , *)
              read (INPUT, graph[i].alt);
              readln (INPUT);
        end;

    close (INPUT);
end;
```

15.3   The List of Document Words

The list of document words is essentially a cache — a list of the words which we have found in the disk dictionary and expect to see again. With any luck, this entire list easily fits in memory and so the only need to access external memory is the first time that each new word is found in the document.

This data structure differs from the list of common words in one major way: the list of document words starts out empty and grows as new words are found. There is no need to delete words from this list (almost). Again, however, we need to be able to search rapidly for a given token.

A hash table is an obvious choice. Our particular favorite is a bucket hash. Given a token, we apply the hash function to compute an index into the hash table. The hash table entry is the head of a chain of entries, each with the same hash value. We search down this chain to find our token. If a null pointer is found, we have reached the end of the chain and the token is not in the list. Thus, our search algorithm is:

```
procedure search_document_words (search_token: search_token_type;
                                 var found: boolean);
    var
        p: hash_chain_index;
        result: compare_result;
    begin
        found := false;
        p := hash_table[hash (search_token)];

        while (p ≠ null) and not found
            do begin
                    (* compare token with word in hash table *)
                    compare (search_token, result, hash_chain[p].word);
                    if result = equal
                        then found := true
                        else p := hash_chain[p].link;
            end;
    end;
```

Now we need to define the hash function and the hash table data structures. The *hash* function should spread the tokens evenly over the *hash_table*. It should be easily computed, although we could trade off some computer time for a more even distribution, leading to a shorter search time. The result of the *hash* function should be a *hash_table_index*.

```
hash_table_index  =  0..hash_table_length;
hash_chain_index  =  0..hash_chain_length;


hash_table:   array [hash_table_index] of hash_chain_index;

hash_chain:   array [hash_chain_index]
                    of record
                              word:   search_token_type;
                              link:   hash_chain_index;
                        end;

n_hash_chain_entries:   hash_chain_index;
```

As a starter, we choose the following hash function, based on the length, first character, and last character of the token.

```
function hash (token:   search_token_type):   hash_table_index;
begin
        hash := (  ((lower_case[token.c[1]] * 29)
                      + lower_case[token.c[token.length]]) * 11
                    + token.length)
                                        mod (hash_table_length + 1);
end;
```

Of course, the length of the hash table (*hash_table_length*+1) should be at least an odd number, preferably relatively prime to 11 and 29, and reasonably large. A prime number in the range 100 to 1000 should do nicely, depending upon memory requirements. We want an average of maybe 10 words per hash chain; each word is say 8 characters long, plus the pointer to the next — about 10 bytes total. Then each hash chain is about 100 bytes. So the number of hash chains can be about *amount_of_memory_for_list_of_document_words*/100.

One other procedure is needed to deal with the list of document words: *add_to_list_of_document_words*. This is straightforward with two considerations.

First, when we add a word onto the appropriate hash chain, do we add it to the beginning or the end of the chain? Since a new word tends to be used again shortly after its first use, we might want to put it at the beginning. On the other hand, words used early in a document are probably used more often than words used later, so maybe we should put a new word at the end. Both approaches have their arguments. For simplicity, we put a new word at the front. However, it appears that we may want to change our search strategy to modify the hash-chains to keep more frequently used words near the front of each hash chain (a self–modifying data structure). This could require a counter in each entry (additional memory overhead). Alternatively, every time we find a word in its hash chain, we can move it one closer to the head of the chain by switching it and the previous entry. Since our list is chained, this is only the change of three pointers. In this way infrequently used words sink to the end of the chain, while frequently used words stay near the top. Another approach would be to always move a newly–found token to the head of its chain.

Statistics on these three data variants of the basic hash table data structure reveal that all of the self–modifying data structures are roughly comparable and considerably better than the static structure. A test of the speller on files of over a half million characters, some 70,000 tokens, required 518,200 token comparison operations for the static structure, while using counters required only 220,100 compares, moving the token up the chain once for every successful find required 205,655 compares, and moving each successfully found token to the front of its chain required 212,223 compares. The exact figures will always vary, but the important fact is that a dynamic data structure reduced the number of comparisons at least in half. (This is an example of the way that minor after the fact modifications can significantly improve the performance of a program.)

The other problem to consider is overflow of the hash table. This problem is easy to detect, but not so easy to correct. We have two options: (1) freeze the list, so that no new words are added, or (2) delete some (hopefully infrequently used) words. Remember that the list of document words is merely acting as a cache, so correct operation does not require it to contain all words in the document; it merely improves performance. Studies (such as the Brown Corpus) show that as many as half of the tokens in a document are used only once. Thus, it would seem that much of the list of document specific words is deadwood and will not be used again. Thus, we favor approach (2) to overflow: delete words.

Now the problem is: which words should be deleted? We want to delete the infrequently used words. The problem is compounded by the representation of tokens. We have so far avoided defining the storage management aspect of the representation of strings. However, we suspect that they will be allocated in a large pool of memory, a *string table*. Entries are added to the string table in the order encountered in the text, not by order of frequency of use. Thus, if we delete the half of the words which are used least frequently, then we delete random strings from all over the string table. This means that the space made available in the table is scattered in randomly sized pieces among randomly sized pieces which are to be retained. This requires either compaction or a memory management policy which is an instance of the dynamic storage allocation problem (first-fit, best-fit, or buddy system).

We propose instead to simply delete *all* words from the list of document words. There are a number of advantages to this approach: (1) it is easy (simply reset a few pointers and counters), (2) it deletes all infrequently used words (among others), (3) it allows easy free space management, and (4) since the list acts as a cache, it does not affect the correct operation of the speller while (5) it definitely eliminates overflow.

With these decisions made, the code is

```
procedure add_to_list_of_document_words (token: token_type);
var
        k:   hash_table_index;
        p:   hash_chain_index;
begin
        (* get hash chain entry *)

        if n_hash_chain_entries ≥ hash_chain_length
           then hash_table_overflow
           else begin
                        (* new hash table entry *)
                        n_hash_chain_entries := n_hash_chain_entries + 1;
                        p := n_hash_chain_entries;

                        (* define new word *)
                        translate_for_search (token, hash_chain[p].word);

                        (* link into hash chain *)
                        k := hash (hash_chain[p].word);
                        hash_chain[p].link := hash_table[k];
                        hash_table[k] := p;
                end;
end;


procedure hash_table_overflow;
var
        i:   hash_table_index;
begin
        (* delete all hash table entries *)

        for i := 0 to hash_table_length
         do hash_table[i] := null;

        n_hash_chain_entries := 0;

end;
```

This overflow procedure can also be used for initialization of the list of document words.

15.4   The Disk Dictionary

This is our major data structure. It's properties are somewhat different from our other lists of words, mainly because of its size. We assume that it is large — so large it

cannot fit in available memory. How then can we search it? We use an indexed
search strategy. The dictionary is stored as a sequence of blocks on a direct access
file. The file is a set of blocks, numbered from 1 to *number_of_dictionary_blocks*.
Each block is of fixed size, probably determined by the operating system as a multiple of the block size supported by the direct access device. (We assume a disk.)
Further, we assume the dictionary is sorted. To access it, we keep a table (an index)
in memory of the first and last words in each block. Then to find a particular word,
we first do a binary search on the index, determining which block of the file should
contain the token. Then we read that block and perform a sequential search of that
block. This two–step search strategy allows us to search the dictionary with at most
one disk read for each new token. The code is basically,

```
procedure search_disk_dictionary (search_token: search_token_type;
                                   var found:  boolean);
var
      block_number:  disk_block_index;
begin
      find_index_of_disk_block (search_token, block_number, found);
      if not found and (block_number ≠ null)
          then search_disk_block (search_token, block_number, found);
end;
```

We consider that the token may be before the first block, after the last block, or fall
between two blocks. Thus the index search may (rarely) reveal that the token is not
in the dictionary, and we need the check for a non–null block number. Note that we
do not *need* both first and last words in a block. Typically the last word in block *i* is
very closely followed by the first word in block *i*+1. By keeping both words, we double our index size but can detect tokens which fall between blocks. If we kept only the
first word per block, or last word per block, we could still search reasonably efficient-
ly.

5.4.1   find_index_block

The index for the dictionary is defined during initialization and consists of an
array of pairs of words. Each pair is the the first word and last word for its block.
Remember the dictionary index is static for the run of the speller.

```
disk_index:  array [1..max_disk_blocks]
                  of record
                              first_word:   search_token_type;
                              last_word:    search_token_type;
                     end;
n_disk_blocks:   0..max_disk_blocks;
```

We use a binary search on the index table.

```
procedure find_index_of_disk_block (search_token: search_token_type;
                                    var block_number: disk_block_index
                                    var found: boolean);
var
        low: disk_block_index;
        mid: disk_block_index;
        high: disk_block_index;
        result: compare_result;
begin
        found := false;
        block_number := null;
        low := 1;
        high := n_disk_blocks;

        (* find the block with first[high] < search_token < first[high+1] *)

        while (high ≥ low) and not found
            do begin
                    mid := (high+low) div 2;

                    compare (search_token, result, disk_index[mid].first_word);
                    case result of

                        less: high := mid - 1;
                        greater: low := mid + 1;
                        equal: begin
                                        block_number := null;
                                        found := true;
                                end;
                    end (* case *);
              end (* while *);

        if not found and (high > 0)
            then begin
                    (* check if first[high] < search_token < last[high] *)

                    compare (search_token, result, disk_index[high].last_word);

                    case result of

                        less: block_number := high;
                        greater: block_number := null;
                        equal: begin
                                        block_number := null;
                                        found := true;
                                end;
                    end (* case *);
               end;
end;
```

5.4.2   *search_block*

Searching a block of the disk dictionary is relatively simple. We first make sure the block is in memory, and then search the block for the token. To get the block into memory, we read it into a buffer. We may have several buffers available, and can use paging techniques to try to keep frequently used buffers in core. Thus, we read the block into one of several buffers, and then search that buffer.

The blocks contain a sequence of words. Each word is separated from the previous word by a *null* character. This *null* character is also used to fill the end of each block. Obviously, the *null* character cannot be allowed to occur within a word; it is a delimiter.

```
procedure search_disk_block (search_token: search_token_type;
                             block_number:  disk_block_index;
                             var found:  boolean);
var
      i:   disk_buff_index;
      j:   token_index;
      k:   0..length_of_disk_block;
begin
      (* get block_number into disk_buffer i *)
      get_disk_block (block_number, i);

      k := 0;
      found := false;
      repeat
            j := 1;
            while (search_token.c[j] = disk_buffer[i][k])
                  and (j ≤ search_token.length)
                do begin
                        j := j + 1;
                        k := k + 1;
                  end;

            if (j = search_token.length+1) and (disk_buffer[i][k]=null)
                then found := true
                else begin (* get on to next word *)
                        while disk_buffer[i][k] ≠ null
                            do k := k + 1;
                        while (disk_buffer[i][k] = null)
                                and (k < length_of_disk_block)
                            do k := k + 1;
                  end;

      until found or (k ≥ length_of_disk_block);
end;
```

15.4.3 get_block

The *get_block* procedure manages the buffers for the disk dictionary disk blocks. We use a least–recently–used (LRU) replacement algorithm, implemented by a doubly–linked list. When a block is used, is taken out of the list and put at the head of the list. When an empty buffer is needed, the buffer at the end is used. We assume that we have *number_of_buffers* buffers numbered starting at 1. The zero element of the doubly–linked list is used for the head and tail pointers.

```
disk_block = array [0..length_of_disk_block] of search_char;
disk_block_index = 0..max_disk_blocks;

disk_buff_index = 0..n_disk_buffers;

n_disk_blocks:  disk_block_index;

disk_buffer:  array [1..n_disk_buffers] of disk_block;

disk_buff_list:  array [disk_buff_index]
                   of record
                          d_block_number:  disk_block_index;
                          forward:  disk_buff_index;
                          backward:  disk_buff_index;
                   end;


procedure get_disk_block (j: disk_block_index; var i: disk_buff_index);
begin
        (* search to see if disk_block j already in a disk_buffer *)

        i := 0;
        repeat
                i := i + 1;
        until (i ≥ n_disk_buffers) or (disk_buff_list[i].d_block_number = j);

        if disk_buff_list[i].d_block_number ≠ j
           then begin (* not in a buffer now, pick LRU and replace *)
                        i := disk_buff_list[0].backward;
                        disk_buff_list[i].d_block_number := j;
                        direct_read (j, disk_buffer[i]);
                end;

        (* disk_block j is in disk_buffer i *)
```

(* take *disk_buffer i* out of doubly–linked list *)

disk_buff_list[*disk_buff_list*[*i*].*backward*].*forward* := *disk_buff_list*[*i*].*forward*;
disk_buff_list[*disk_buff_list*[*i*].*forward*].*backward* := *disk_buff_list*[*i*].*backward*;

(* put at front of list *)
disk_buff_list[*i*].*forward* := *disk_buff_list*[0].*forward*;
disk_buff_list[*i*].*backward* := 0;

disk_buff_list[*disk_buff_list*[*i*].*forward*].*backward* := *i*;
disk_buff_list[0].*forward* := *i*;
    end;

The *direct_read* procedure is system dependent, and not a part of most standard languages. However, it is needed in whatever language this program is implemented in. We need to read block *j* from the disk dictionary into *buffer*[*i*].

These last routines complete the search procedures to try to find a given token in the dictionary. We have seen how a three level dictionary structure can be used to speed the checking of a token. Now the problem is simply what to do with the tokens which are not found in the dictionary. In our program so far, this function is handled by the routine *ask_user_about_it*.

16.0   What To Do With Misspelled Tokens

We have found a token which is not in the dictionary. In both a spelling checker and a spelling corrector, we now display the error for the user and ask what should be done. The only difference between a checker and a corrector is whether we attempt to find a list of candidate correct spellings before asking the user for a command.

procedure *ask_user_about_it* (**var** *token*: *token_type*);
begin
    guess_index := 0;
    if *mode.correct*
        then *find_candidates* (*token*);

    display_context;
    display_token (*token*);
    writeln (*TTYO*, ‘ ?’);

    read_and_obey_table_2_command (*token*);
    end;

16.1   display_context

At this point, we assume a very simple form of context display: we simply write the entire context. Actually, we only want to write the context once, so we introduce a boolean variable *context_is_displayed* which is set false whenever the context changes (in *reset_regions*) and true whenever the context is displayed. In a more advanced system, we might want to update the context on the screen dynamically, using cursor movements to change the screen contents. This affects only this one module of the speller.

```
procedure display_context;
var
      i:   line_number;
      j:   line_index;
begin
      if not context_is_displayed
          then for i := 1 to n_lines
              do begin
                      for j := 1 to context_buffer[i].length
                          do display_character (context_buffer[i].c[j]);
                      j := context_buffer[i].length;
                      if context_buffer[i].c[j] ≠ end_of_line
                          then writeln (TTYO);
              end;

      context_is_displayed := true;
end;
```

Displaying the token is also easy.

```
procedure display_token (token: token_type);
var
      j:   token_index;
begin
      for j := 1 to token.length
          do display_character (token.c[j]);
end;
```

Both of these routines must display characters on the screen. But displaying one character may require several display characters (for example, control characters). So this is isolated into a separate *display_character* procedure.

```
procedure display_character (c: pseudo_char);
var
      k:   0..2;
begin
```

```
        if c = end_of_line
           then writeln (TTYO)
           else for k := 1 to display_form[c].length
                 do write (TTYO, display_form[c].representation[k]);
   end;
```

16.2   find_candidates

Now we need to design the spelling correction procedures. These procedures are considered by most people to be the most important part of the spelling program, and have certainly been the subject of the most research. We isolate our algorithms inside this one procedure, find_candidates. The interface is quite simple. The input is a token which is believed to be misspelled (we can not find it in the dictionary); the output should be a list of possible correct spellings. Any algorithm or collection of algorithms we wish may be used to generate the list.

```
candidate_table_index = 0..max_candidate_list_length;

n_candidates:  candidate_table_index;
candidate:  array [candidate_table_index] of token_type;
```

Since we are most interested in the general design problem, we use the standard correction algorithms here. This assumes that a spelling error results from one (and only one) of the following four errors:

1.   transposed letters

2.   one extra letter

3.   one wrong letter

4.   one missing letter

Thus our procedure is simply,

```
procedure find_candidates (token: token_type);
begin
      n_candidates := 0;

      try_transposed_letters (token);
      try_extra_letter (token);
      try_wrong_letter (token);
      try_missing_letter (token);

      guess_correct_spelling;
end;
```

The variable *n_candidates* indicates the number of possible correct spellings on our list. Each time we find a new candidate we call the following procedure to add it to our list.

```
procedure new_candidate (token: token_type);
begin
        if n_candidates < max_candidate_list_length
            then begin
                        n_candidates := n_candidates + 1;
                        candidate[n_candidates] := token;
                end;
end;
```

At this point, we are not sure how expensive (in terms of computer time) the correction procedures will be, so we design them in the most straightforward manner. These procedures produce all tokens which can lead to the given token under the suspected error, and search for these new tokens in the dictionary. If the new token is found, then it is a candidate spelling and is added to the list of candidates.

16.2.1   *guess_correct_spelling*

From the list of candidate spellings, many spellers will try to "guess" the correct spelling. This can be most impressive to new users when care is taken in the guessing procedure. The guess algorithm can be quite complex, maintaining a history of the types of spelling errors made by this particular user and using this profile to identify the most likely correct spelling.

The speller can be almost as successful, however, by using a much simpler guessing rule. We guess a spelling only when exactly one candidate spelling has been found. If we guess (and we will not guess all the time), then we display the guess to the user and set the variable *guess_index* to point to the guessed word (in the candidate list). If we do not guess, *guess_index* is zero.

```
procedure guess_correct_spelling;
begin
        if n_candidates = 1
            then guess_index := 1
            else guess_index := 0;
end;
```

To display a guess, we simply,

```
procedure display_guess;
begin
        if guess_index ≠ 0
            then begin
                        write (TTYO, 'I guess:   ');
```

```
                        display_token (candidate[guess_index]);
                        writeln (TTYO);
                end;
        end;
```

16.2.2   try_transposed_letters

We first need to copy the token to a working variable area. Then we produce
each token which can produce the given token by transposing letters. Since transposing letters is a self–inverting operation, we simply transpose each adjacent pair of
letters in the original token. If we look at a simple example, we see that for a token
abcd, we need to generate the tokens,

bacd	(transpose a, b)
acbd	(transpose b, c)
abdc	(transpose c, d)

Noting which letters stay constant and which are modified, we can generate these
tokens by the following code. For each generated token, we search the dictionary. If
the token is found, we add it to the list of candidate spellings.

```
procedure try_transposed_letters (token: token_type);
var
        c:  pseudo_char;
        i:  token_index;
        new_token:  token_type;
        found:  boolean;
begin
        new_token := token;

        (* exchange letters *)
        i := 1;
        c := new_token.c[1];

        while i < token.length
            do begin
                        new_token.c[i] := new_token.c[i+1];
                        new_token.c[i+1] := c;

                        search_dictionary (new_token, found);
                        if found
                            then new_candidate (new_token);

                        (* generate next token *)
                        i := i + 1;
                        c := new_token.c[i-1];
                        new_token.c[i-1] := new_token.c[i];
                end;
        end;
```

16.2.3   *try_extra_letter*

For this procedure, we assume that an extra letter has been added to the correct word to give our misspelled token. To correct this, we delete each letter of the token and search for the resulting token.

Again, we examine an example. For the given token *abcd*, we must generate,

bcd	(delete *a*)
acd	(delete *b*)
abd	(delete *c*)
abc	(delete *d*)

This results in the following code. First shift the token left one character, as it is copied into our working token space and then restore the token, one letter at a time.

```
procedure try_extra_letter (token: token_type);
var
        i:  token_index;
        new_token:  token_type;
        found:  boolean;
begin
        for i := 1 to token.length - 1
          do new_token.c[i] := token.c[i+1];
        new_token.length := token.length - 1;

        for i := 1 to token.length
          do begin
                   search_dictionary (new_token, found);
                   if found
                       then new_candidate (new_token);

                   new_token.c[i] := token.c[i];
              end;
end;
```

16.2.4   *try_wrong_letter and try_missing_letter*

The above two procedures are relatively fast since they work with the existing letters. The next two must try to come up with new letters. If one letter is missing, we can treat that as a token of one more character in length with the inserted character being wrong. Thus these two procedures have a common sub-procedure which checks a specific position in the token for a wrong letter. Using this common sub-procedure, we have,

```
procedure try_wrong_letter (token: token_type);
var
      i:  token_index;
      new_token:  token_type;
begin
      new_token := token;

      for i := 1 to new_token.length
        do try_one_letter_wrong_at (i, new_token);
end;
```

For a missing letter, we try each position, one after another, as the position of
the missing letter. Thus, initially, we copy the token into our work space shifted right
one letter. We use a null character to represent the missing character, since we don't
know what it should be.

```
procedure try_missing_letter (token: token_type);
var
      i:  token_index;
      new_token:  token_type;
begin
      new_token.length := token.length + 1;
      for i := 1 to token.length
        do new_token.c[i+1] := token.c[i];

      for i := 1 to new_token.length
        do begin
                new_token.c[i] := null;
                try_one_letter_wrong_at (i, new_token);
                new_token.c[i] := token.c[i];
           end;
end;
```

To check if we have one letter wrong, in position i, we replace that letter with each
possible alternate letter, except, of course, the current value.

```
procedure try_one_letter_wrong_at (i: token_index; new_token: token_type);
var
      old_c:  pseudo_char;
      c:  pseudo_char;
      found:  boolean;
begin
      old_c := new_token.c[i];

      for c := ord('a') to ord('z')
        do if c ≠ old_c
```

```
                        then begin
                                new_token.c[i] := c;
                                search_dictionary (new_token, found);
                                if found
                                    then new_candidate (new_token);
                        end;

                new_token.c[i] := old_c;  (* restore *)
        end;
```

We have deliberately not considered either numeric characters nor the apostrophe in this code, thinking them to be infrequently used.

17.0   What To Do With Misspelled Tokens (continued)

Once we have displayed the token and its context and generated all possible candidate spellings, we must actually ask the user what to do. This is an opportunity to reuse our procedure for reading user commands (*get_command*).

The types of commands possible include:

help: list available commands.

accept: the token is correctly spelled in this context (but may not be in other contexts).

insert: the token is correctly spelled in this and all other contexts. Add it to the local dictionary for this file.

replace: the token is wrong; replace it with a new token in this context. The user specifies the new token.

substitute: the token is wrong and should be uniformly replaced throughout the remainder of the text. The user specifies the new token.

edit: the text is thoroughly messed up and the user wants to correct it manually.

These are the basic commands. In addition there are some useful control functions which might be provided whenever a (potentially) misspelled token is found.

quit: Something terrible has happened; abort the session and return to the operating system at once.

skip: the remainder of the text should just be copied; the user either knows it is correct, or doesn't care, or doesn't have the time to correct it now.

load, dump, clear: The user may decide that the dictionary should be modified.

mode: The user may want to change some mode settings, especially those controlling the definition of a token.

display: After all the above changes, we may have forgotten the suspect token which is under consideration; mainly only a problem for CRT displays.

In addition, if we are in a correcting mode (*mode.correct* is true) and have found suitable candidate correct spellings (*n_candidates* > 0), we may have the following additional commands.

correct: the speller "guessed" a correct spelling, and was right. The generated correct spelling should replace the misspelled token. (Should the replacement be similar to a *replace* command or a *substitute* command?)

list: If there are several alternate candidate spellings, the user may want to see all of them and select one of them.

Note that not all of the above commands resolve the problem of what to do with the current token. Only *accept, insert, replace, substitute, quit, correct* and (maybe) *edit* indicate what to do; the others simply change the environment of the speller to reflect a change in the needs of the user. Thus our general structure must allow us to repeatedly read (and execute) commands until we know what to do about this token. This introduces a local variable *complete* which is true if we have finished with this token, and false otherwise. We loop until *complete* is true.

```
procedure read_and_obey_table_2_command (var token: token_type);
var
        complete:  boolean;
        cmd:  command;
begin
        repeat (* until complete *)

                get_command (cmd, table_2);
                complete := true;

                case cmd of

                        help:  begin
                                list_commands (table_2);
```

```
                                complete := false;
          end;

quit:   mode.quit := true;

skip:   mode.skip := true;

accept:   begin (* no action necessary *) end;

insert:   insert_token (token);

replace:   replace_token (token);

substitute:   substitute_token (token);

edit:   edit_context;

clear:   begin
                    clear_local_dictionary;
                    complete := false;
            end;

load:   begin
                    load_local_dictionary;
                    complete := false;
            end;

dump:   begin
                    dump_local_dictionary;
                    complete := false;
            end;

mode:   begin
                    set_modes;
                    complete := false;
            end;

display:   begin
                        context_is_displayed := false;
                        display_context;
                        display_token (token);
                        writeln (TTYO, ' ?');
                        display_guess;
                        complete := false;
                end;
```

```
                correct:  replace_with_candidate (complete);


            list:  begin
                              list_candidates;
                              complete := false;
                    end;


                statistics:  write_statistics;


            end (* case *);


        until complete;
end;
```

We must create a new command table, *table_2*, and initialize it.

```
table_2:  command_table;

procedure table_2_initialize;
begin
      table_2.prompt := '?';
      table_2.next := null;

      enter_command_table (table_2, help, 'help ');
      enter_command_table (table_2, quit, 'quit ');
      enter_command_table (table_2, quit, 'exit ');
      enter_command_table (table_2, skip, 'skip ');
      enter_command_table (table_2, accept, 'accept ');
      enter_command_table (table_2, insert, 'insert ');
      enter_command_table (table_2, replace, 'replace ');
      enter_command_table (table_2, substitute, 'substitute ');
      enter_command_table (table_2, edit, 'edit ');
      enter_command_table (table_2, clear, 'clear ');
      enter_command_table (table_2, load, 'load ');
      enter_command_table (table_2, dump, 'dump ');
      enter_command_table (table_2, mode, 'mode ');
      enter_command_table (table_2, display, 'display ');
      enter_command_table (table_2, correct, 'correct ');
      enter_command_table (table_2, list, 'list ');
      enter_command_table (table_2, statistics, 'statistics ');
end;
```

The implementation of these user commands is generally straightforward.

The *help* command lists the command table.

The *quit* and *skip* commands set mode flags which can also be set directly by the *mode* command.

The *mode* command allows any of the mode switches to be set or reset.

The dictionary manipulation routines call the appropriate procedures just as for top–level commands.

The *display* command displays the token and its context.

The *accept* command results in no work.

The other commands require new procedures to be designed and written. We now examine these procedures.

17.1 insert_token

When the command is *insert*, we must *accept* the token and also add it to the local and disk dictionaries. This is accomplished by,

```
procedure insert_token (token: token_type);
begin
      add_to_inserted_word_buffer (token);
end;
```

This procedure is discussed more in the section on local dictionary manipulation.

17.2 list_candidates

Listing the candidate spellings is quite simple, requiring only formatting thought. Candidates can be printed in columns across the display, or simply one per line. We choose the latter for simplicity.

```
procedure list_candidates;
var
      i:  candidate_table_index;
begin
      if n_candidates ≤ 0
          then writeln (TTYO, 'No candidates found')
          else for i := 1 to n_candidates
                do begin
                        write (TTYO, i:4, '  ');
                        display_token (candidate[i]);
                        writeln (TTYO);
                  end;
```

```
          if n_candidates ≠ 1
              then guess_index := 0;
    end;
```

17.3   replace_with_candidate

Two situations can arise here. First, we may have guessed the correct spelling, and should use that guess. Second, we may have a list of candidates and the user wants us to replace the token with one of those. the problem is how to distinguish these two situations. Since we know that we are guessing only when there is only one candidate, we distinguish on the basis of *guess_index*. If *guess_index* is non–zero, we replace with the guessed candidate word; if *guess_index* is zero, we ask the user to specify the index of the candidate to use. An illegal index (0, for example) will cause us to return to the command interpreter with *complete* false.

```
procedure replace_with_candidate (var complete: boolean);
begin
        if guess_index = 0
            then begin
                        write (TTYO, 'Which candidate number?');
                        readln (TTYI, guess_index);
                end;

        if (0 < guess_index) and (guess_index ≤ n_candidates)
            then token := candidate[guess_index]
            else complete := false;
end;
```

17.4   replace and substitute

These two commands are quite similar. Both require reading a new token from the user and using it instead of the current token. The only difference between them is that *substitute* must remember the new token and use it whenever the old token should occur in the text in the future. This leads to the following procedures:

```
procedure replace_token (var token: token_type);
var
        new_token:  token_type;
begin
        write (TTYO, 'Replace with:   ');
        read_new_token (new_token);
        token := new_token;
end;
```

```
procedure substitute_token (var token: token_type);
var
      new_token:  token_type;
begin
      write (TTYO, 'Substitute throughout with:   ');
      read_new_token (new_token);
      remember (token, new_token);
      token := new_token;
end;


procedure read_new_token (var new_token: token_type);
var
      j:  token_index;
      c:  char;
begin
      j := 0;
      while not eoln (TTYI)
         do begin
                    j := j + 1;
                    read (TTYI, c);
                    new_token.c[j] := ord(c);
              end;
      readln (TTYI);
      new_token.length := j;
end;
```

17.4.1   remember, old and new

The *remember* function requires some modification to previous code. The problem is quite simple: we are given two tokens, *old* and *new* and need to automatically replace all occurrences of *old* with *new* in the future text. This requires a new table: the *substitution_table* of (*old*, *new*) pairs. The *remember* procedure merely adds a new pair to this table. For the moment, let us use a simple linear list for the table:

```
substitution_table_index = 0..max_substitution_table_length;

n_substitution_table:  substitution_table_index;
substitution_table:    array [substitution_table_index]
                          of record
                                   old:  token_type;
                                   new:  token_type;
                              end;
```

```
procedure remember (old: token_type; new: token_type);
begin
      n_substitution_table := n_substitution_table + 1;
      substitution_table[n_substitution_table].old := old;
      substitution_table[n_substitution_table].new := new;
end;
```

However, to use this table, we need to change one of our existing procedures to search this table whenever a token is found. Several opportunities exist for this search:

> check_spelling,
> get_token,
> search_dictionary,
> ask_user_about_it,
> or output_token.

We would not want the substitution to occur in output_token since although we may want all occurrences of "old" replaced by "new", we may also want some other token replaced by "old". Search_dictionary is also a bad choice since intuitively it should be side-effect-free, and is also used to generate candidate spellings. We like the current looks of check_spelling and feel that adding a search of the sub-stitution_table would clutter it. There is a certain beauty in adding the search and substitution to get_token since this would allow the new token to be checked for spelling errors, too. However, we feel that semantically the desired function is to simply bypass asking the user what to do in the future by generating an automatic replace command. Thus the appropriate place is in ask_user_about_it. We change this procedure to:

```
procedure ask_user_about_it (var token: token_type);
var
      complete:  boolean;
begin
      check_for_generated_command (token, complete);
      if not complete
        then begin
                  guess_index := 0;
                  if mode.correct
                     then find_candidates (token);

                  display_context;
                  display_token (token);
                  writeln (TTYO, ' ?');
                  display_guess;

                  read_and_obey_table_2_command (token);
             end;
end;
```

Notice that *complete* is being used to indicate whether a command was automatically generated and executed. Our new *check_for_generated_command* procedure is:

```
procedure check_for_generated_command (var token: token_type;
                                        var complete:  boolean);
var
      i:  substitution_table_index;
      found:  boolean;
begin
      complete := false;

      search_substitution_table (token, i, found);
      if found
         then begin
                    complete := true;
                    token := substitution_table[i].new;
              end;
end;
```

Assuming that the *substitution_table* will be small, we use a linear search.

```
procedure search_substitution_table (token: token_type;
                                     var i:  substitution_table_index;
                                     var found:  boolean);
var
      result:  compare_result;
begin
      i := n_substitution_table;
      found := false;

      while (0 < i) and not found
         do begin
                  compare (token, result, substitution_table[i].old);
                  if result = equal
                     then found := true
                     else i := i - 1;
              end;
end;
```

18.0   Local Dictionaries

A local dictionary feature allows the user to augment the shared master dictionary with words which are local to the subject area or author. The user-specified local dictionaries are merged with the master dictionary to create the direct access disk dictionary for the *search_dictionary* procedure.

The following local dictionary operations are defined:

    (1) *load*: a user-specified file of words is added to the disk-dictionary.

    (2) *dump*: a list of all words added to the disk-dictionary is copied to a
user-specified file.

    (3) *clear*: the list of words added to the disk dictionary is set empty.

In addition there is the implicit addition to the local dictionary of the insert command of *table_2*.

    (4) *insert*: add a new token to the disk dictionary.

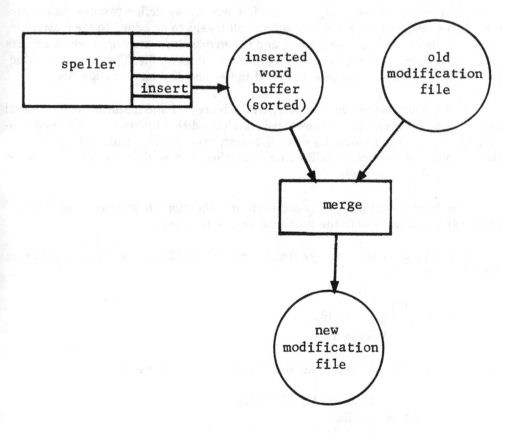

Figure 6. Production of a new modification file from an old modification file and a buffer of sorted words.

The relationship of the load command to the insert command can be made more obvious by describing the load command as follows:

(1) *load*: insert each token in a user-specified local dictionary file.

Thus the problem of loading a local dictionary can be reduced to adding one token at a time to the disk dictionary, in the same manner as our handling of the *insert* command.

The disk dictionary is quite large and modifying it in place might be difficult; it would be necessary to define overflow disk blocks and severely complicate our disk search algorithm. Therefore, we prefer to batch our additions to the disk dictionary. When enough additions exist, we merge all of them into the disk dictionary, creating a new disk dictionary.

We also need a file which lists the tokens added to the disk dictionary; this provides a source for the dump command. Therefore we define two new data structures: (1) a *modification file* which collects all tokens to be added to the master dictionary to define the disk dictionary, and (2) an *inserted word buffer* which collects all inserted words until they are added to the modification file. The current local dictionary is the union of the inserted word buffer and the modification file.

Figure 6 shows how the modification file is created and maintained. The initial modification file is empty. Whenever we search the disk dictionary and the modification file has changed since the disk dictionary was created (from the master dictionary and the previous modification file) then a new disk dictionary must be created (as shown in Figure 7).

The dump command simply copies the modification file to a user-specified file. The clear command resets the modification file to empty.

With this discussion, we see that we need three files for loading and changing the modification file:

    user file
    old modification file
    new modification file

and when we create the direct access disk dictionary, we need,

    master dictionary (MASTER.DIC)
    modification file
    direct access disk dictionary (DISK.DIC)

The modification files are temporary files created by the spelling program; we must be sure not to use the same file names as user files. Two solutions are possible.

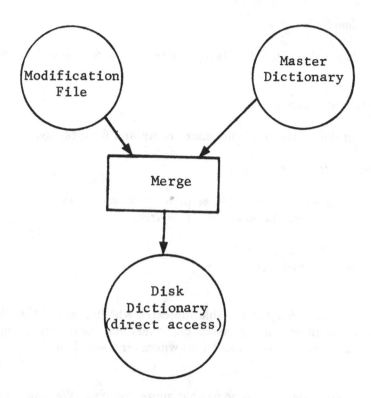

Figure 7. Creation of the disk dictionary from the master dictionary and a modification file.

On some systems, the operating system will provide, upon request, file names guaranteed to be unique. In this case, we can simply ask the system for a new file name whenever necessary. The other solution is to notice that although there may be many modification files, only the most recent one is of interest (or the most recent two while an old one is being used to make a new one). Thus, we can operate with no more than two file names for the modification files. These file names can be picked for their obscurity (unlikely to be chosen by the user) and then publicized as being used by the speller. If the user has files of these names, they may well be destroyed by the speller.

Now to keep track of the two modification files, we define an array of their file names.

    mod_file: **array** [1..2] **of** *filename*;

and a variable *current_mod_file* to identify the current modification file. The initial state, of no modification file, can either be produced by creating an empty file, or by encoding *current_mod_file* with a special value. We prefer the latter, and so, *current_mod_file*: 0..2;

where an initial value of 0 indicates that there is no current modification file.

18.1   *clear* and *dump*

We can define the local dictionary command for clear by,

procedure *clear_local_dictionary*;
begin
      if (*current_mod_file* ≠ 0) **or** (*n_inserted_word* ≠ 0)
        then *mod_file_has_changed* := *true*;

      current_mod_file := 0;
      clear_inserted_word_buffer;
end;

The *mod_file_has_changed* variable indicates whether or not the disk dictionary must be created anew from the master dictionary and the (newly changed) modification file. This must be checked and done whenever a search of the disk dictionary occurs.

The dump command is somewhat more complex. We must first merge any words in the *inserted_word_buffer* into the current modification file, and then copy this file to a user specified new local file.

procedure *dump_local_dictionary*;
var
      c: *char*;
      file_name: *filename*;
begin
      write (*TTYO*, 'Output file name: ');
      readln (*TTYI*, *file_name*);
      rewrite (*LOCAL_OUT*, *file_name*);

      flush_inserted_word_buffer;

      if *current_mod_file* ≠ 0
        then begin
              reset (*LOCAL_IN*, *mod_file*[*current_mod_file*]);
              while not *eof* (*LOCAL_IN*)
                do begin
                    read (*LOCAL_IN*, *c*);
                    write (*LOCAL_OUT*, *c*);
                end;
              close (*LOCAL_IN*);
        end;

```
        close (LOCAL_OUT);
end;
```

18.2   load_local_dictionary

To load a local dictionary, we read and insert each token in the user-specified file. Again, we have the problem of deciding what is a token, but we ignore the details here and simply collect all non-delimiters between delimiters. Thus, we have,

```
procedure load_local_dictionary;
var
        token:   token_type;
        c:   pseudo_char;
        cc:   char;
        file_name:   filename;
begin
        write (TTYO, 'Load file name:   ');
        readln (TTYI, file_name);
        reset (USER, file_name);

        while not eof (USER)
            do begin
                    repeat
                            read (USER, cc);
                            c := ord(cc);
                    until eof (USER) or not (class[c] = delimiter);

                    if not eof (USER)
                        then begin
                                    collect_user_token (c, token);
                                    if token.length > 0
                                        then add_to_inserted_word_buffer (token);
                                end;
                end;

        close (USER);
end;
```

18.2.1   collect_user_token

The collect_user_token procedure simply reads non-tokens from the user file until a delimiter is encountered (or end of file). If the input token exceeds the maximum token length, it is discarded by setting the returned token.length to zero.

```
    procedure collect_user_token (var c: pseudo_char; var token: token_type);
    var
        j:  token_index;
        cc:  char;
    begin
        j := 0;
        while (class[c] ≠ delimiter) and (j < max_token_length)
            do begin
                    j := j + 1;
                    token.c[j] := c;

                    if eof (USER)
                        then c := end_of_file
                        else begin
                                read (USER, cc);
                                c := ord(cc);
                            end;
                end;

        if class[c] = delimiter
            then token.length := j
            else begin
                    token.length := 0;
                    while class[c] ≠ delimiter
                        do if eof (USER)
                                then c := end_of_file
                                else begin
                                        read (USER, cc);
                                        c := ord(cc);
                                    end;
                end;

    end;
```

18.3   The Inserted Word Buffer

The inserted word buffer is used to hold inserted words until they are merged into the modification file. It has three operations,

(1) *clear_inserted_word_buffer*: set the buffer empty.

(2) *add_to_inserted_word_buffer*: add a new token to the buffer,

(3) *flush_inserted_word_buffer*: merge the buffer to the current modification file, producing a new modification file.

To facilitate the merging operation, we keep the inserted word buffer sorted. Since words are added one at a time to this sorted buffer, we use an insertion sort. Since many insertions will be from local dictionary files which are derived from modification files, which are sorted, we expect many words to be inserted in sorted order. Thus we insert from the rear. However, we remove for merging from the front. Rather than move words as we insert, we use a linked list.

It would appear that we need two links for this data structure, a forward link to allow removing words one at a time from the front, and a backward link to allow inserting words one at a time from the back. However, note that we do not need to insert or remove in random order. Rather we repeatedly insert, starting from an empty list, until we must flush the list. Then we repeatedly remove until the list is empty.

Thus, we do not need links in both directions at the same time. This allows us to use only one link. While words are being inserted, this link points backwards, from back to front. when we want to remove words, we reverse the links so that they now point from the front to the rear. Then iems are removed from the front, by following the links, until the list is empty.

To follow the links, we need a *head* pointer (which sometimes points to the front and sometimes to the rear), and the buffer itself. To simplify the insertion sort, we let the head be element 0 of our buffer.

inserted_word_index = 0..*max_inserted_word*;

n_inserted_word: *inserted_word_index*;
inserted_word_buffer: **array** [*inserted_word_index*]
                                of record
                                            link: *inserted_word_index*;
                                            word: *token_type*;
                        end;

Now our three procedures operate on this data structure. *clear_inserted_word_buffer* simply sets *head* to null. (We may want to reclaim storage here — we consider this later when we design the storage management for our speller.)

```
procedure clear_inserted_word_buffer;
begin
        n_inserted_word := 0;
        inserted_word_buffer[0].link := 0;
    end;
```

18.3.1   add_to_inserted_word_buffer

The add_to_inserted_word_buffer procedure is equally simple with the observation that when the buffer is full, we call flush_inserted_word_buffer to merge it with the current modification file.

```
procedure add_to_inserted_word_buffer (token: token_type);
begin
      if n_inserted_word ≥ max_inserted_word
        then flush_inserted_word_buffer;
      insert_sorted (token);
      add_to_list_of_document_words (token);
end;
```

18.3.2   insert_sorted

The insertion sort is very simple.

```
procedure insert_sorted (token: token_type);
var
        p:  inserted_word_index;
        last:  inserted_word_index;
        result:  compare_result;
begin
        p := 0;
        repeat
                last := p;
                p := inserted_word_buffer[p].link;
                if p = null
                    then result := greater
                    else compare (token, result, inserted_word_buffer[p].word);
        until (result ≠ less);

        if result = greater
            then begin
                        n_inserted_word := n_inserted_word + 1;
                        inserted_word_buffer[n_inserted_word].word := token;
                        inserted_word_buffer[n_inserted_word].link := p;
                        inserted_word_buffer[last].link := n_inserted_word;
                end;

end;
```

Notice that this sort does not insert duplicates.

8.3.3   flush_inserted_word_buffer

To merge the inserted word buffer with the modification file, we first reverse our linked list, and then merge the old modification file with the resulting sorted linked list, to produce a new modification file.

```
procedure flush_inserted_word_buffer;
begin
        if n_inserted_word > 0
            then begin
                        reverse_linked_list;
                        merge_with_modification_file;
                 end;
            inserted_word_buffer[0].link := null;
end;
```

To reverse the linked list we simply follow the links, reversing as we go.

```
procedure reverse_linked_list;
var
        last:  inserted_word_index;
        p:  inserted_word_index;
        q:  inserted_word_index;
begin
        last := 0;
        p := inserted_word_buffer[last].link (* head *);
        while p ≠ null
            do begin
                        q := inserted_word_buffer[p].link;
                        inserted_word_buffer[].link := last;
                        last := p;
                        p := q;
                 end;

        inserted_word_buffer[0].link := last;
end;
```

8.3.4   merge_with_modification_file

To merge the list of inserted words with the modification file is a fairly straightforward problem. Each of our two sources (the linked list and the old modification file) produces one token at a time when the previous token from that source is processed. The two tokens are compared and the smaller is output. If the tokens are equal, the new one in the inserted word list is discarded.

```
     procedure merge_with_modification_file;
     var
           p:  new_word_index;
           search_token:  search_token_type;
           result:  compare_result;
     begin
         set_up_mod_files;
         p := inserted_word_buffer[0].link;
         get_next_from_mod_file (token, end_of_mod_file);
         while (p ≠ null) or not end_of_mod_file
             do begin
                     if p = null
                         then result := less
                     else if end_of_mod_file
                         then result := greater
                     else compare (token, result, inserted_word_buffer[p].word);

                     case result of

                         less:  begin
                                     write_mod_token (token);
                                     get_next_from_mod_file (token, end_of_mod_file);
                                 end;

                         equal:  p := inserted_word_buffer[p].link;

                         greater:  begin
                                     write_mod_token (inserted_word_buffer[p].word);
                                     p := inserted_word_buffer[p].link;
                                 end;

                     end (* case *);
             end;

         reset_mod_files;
     end;
```

Now we have minor procedures to write to fill in the details. To set up the modification files, we open two files, MOD_IN and MOD_OUT as appropriate according to *current_mod_file*.

```
     procedure set_up_mod_files;
     var
           next:  1..2;
     begin
         if current_mod_file = 1
             then next := 2
             else next := 1;
```

```
     if current_mod_file = 0
        then end_of_mod_file := true
        else begin
                    reset (MOD_IN, mod_file[current_mod_file]);
                    end_of_mod_file := eof (MOD_IN);
              end;

     rewrite (MOD_OUT, mod_file[next]);
 end;
```

To get the next token from the modification file, we skip any leading delimiters and collect the non–delimiter sequence. Since modification files are produced only by the speller from this same session, we need not consider tokens which exceed *max. _token_length*.

```
procedure get_next_from_mod_file (var token: token_type;
                                  var end_of_mod_file:  boolean);
begin
      if not end_of_mod_file
        then begin
                  c := null;
                  while (class[c] = delimiter) and not eof (MOD_IN)
                     do begin
                              read (MOD_IN, cc);
                              c := ord(cc);
                        end;

                  if eof (MOD_IN)
                     then end_of_mod_file := true
                     else begin
                              j := 0;
                              repeat
                                    j := j + 1;
                                    token.c[j] := c;
                                    read (MOD_IN, cc);
                                    c := ord(cc);
                              until (class[c]=delimiter) or eof (MOD_IN);

                              token.length := j;
                        end;
              end;
 end;
```

To write a token to the new mod file is simply,

```
procedure write_mod_token (token: token_type);
const
      CR = 13;
      LF = 10;
var
      j: token_index;
begin
      for j := 1 to token.length
        do write (MOD_OUT, chr(token.c[j]));
      write (MOD_OUT, chr(CR));
      write (MOD_OUT, chr(LF));
end;
```

Finally, we reset the files at the end of copying by,

```
procedure reset_mod_files;
begin
      close (MOD_IN);
      close (MOD_OUT);

      if current_mod_file = 1
         then current_mod_file := 2
         else current_mod_file := 1;

      mod_file_has_changed := true;
end;
```

18.4   Creating the Disk Dictionary

The *mod_file_has_changed* variable is set whenever the current modification file is replaced by a new one. If the modification file has changed, then we must redefine the disk dictionary before its next use. The easiest way to do this is to modify *search_disk_dictionary*. We only use the disk dictionary in this procedure, so we change it to,

```
procedure search_disk_dictionary (search_token: search_token_type;
                                   var found:  boolean);
var
      block_number:  disk_block_index;
begin
      if mod_file_has_changed
         then define_disk_dictionary;

      find_index_of_disk_block (search_token, block_number, found);
      if not found and (block_number ≠ null)
         then search_disk_block (search_token, block_number, found);
end;
```

One side benefit of this approach is that initialization of the disk dictionary now becomes simply a matter of setting *current_mod_file* to zero, and *mod_file_has_changed* to true. Then when the initial attempt is made to access the disk dictionary, it will automatically be created.

8.4.1   define_disk_dictionary

The *define_disk_dictionary* procedure creates the disk dictionary by merging the master dictionary and the modification file as shown in Figure 7. These two input files are merged and written to the direct access disk dictionary. As the disk dictionary is created, the disk index *disk_index* must be defined. Thus, our *define_disk_dictionary* is,

```
procedure define_disk_dictionary;
var
        end_of_input:  boolean;
        token:  token_type;
begin
        flush_inserted_word_buffer;
        set_up_for_disk_creation (end_of_input);

        while not end_of_input
           do begin
                        get_next_merged_token (token, end_of_input);
                        if not end_of_input
                           then output_token_to_disk_dictionary (token);
             end;

        finish_disk_dictionary_creation;
end;
```

We flush the inserted word buffer to assure that the modification file is up–to–date.

Now to set–up the two input files for reading, we,

```
procedure set_up_for_disk_creation (var end_of_input: boolean);
begin
        if current_mod_file = 0
           then end_of_mod_file := true
           else begin
                        reset (MOD_IN, mod_file[current_mod_file]);
                        end_of_mod_file := false;
                        get_next_from_mod_file (mod_token, end_of_mod_file);
             end;

        reset (MASTER, 'MASTER.DIC');
        end_of_master_file := false;
        get_next_from_master_file (master_token, end_of_master_file);
```

> $end\_of\_input := end\_of\_mod\_file$ **and** $end\_of\_master\_file$;

In addition, we need to set–up for the construction of the disk index and the direct access disk dictionary file, DICT. We will be putting tokens into buffers, one at a time until the buffer is full, then writing the entire buffer to the file and defining the *disk_index* entry for this block. Thus, we need a variable to step through the *disk_index*, (*n_disk_blocks*), a variable to indicate the buffer we are using (*current_buffer*) and a variable to keep track of the next available spot in the buffer (*next*). These are then initialized by,

> $rewrite\ (DICT,\ \text{`DISK.DIC'});$
> $n\_disk\_blocks := 0;$
> $current\_buffer := 1;$
> $next := 0;$
> **end**;

18.4.2   Merge Modification File and Master File

Now to get the next token from either the modification file or the master file, we have a variant on the merge procedure we have already written.

```
procedure get_next_merged_token (var token: token_type;
                                 var end_of_input:  boolean);
var
     result:  compare_result;
begin
     if end_of_master_file
         then if end_of_mod_file
                 then end_of_input := true
                 else result := less
         else if end_of_mod_file
                 then result := greater
                 else compare (mod_token, result, master_token);

     if not end_of_input
       then case result of

     less:  begin
                token := mod_token;
                get_next_from_mod_file (mod_token, end_of_mod_file);
            end;

     equal:  begin
                token := mod_token;
                get_next_from_mod_file (mod_token, end_of_mod_file);
                get_next_from_master_file (master_token, end_of_master_file);
             end;
```

```
        greater:   begin
                       token := master_token;
                       get_next_from_master_file (master_token, end_of_master_file);
                   end;

          end (* case *);
  end;
```

We notice now that the *get_next_from_mod_file* and *get_nex-*
_from_master_file are the same except for the file to be read. Thus, we rewrite our
existing *get_next_from_mod_file* to parameterize the file name as:

```
procedure get_next_from_file (FILE: text;
                                  var token:  token_type;
                                  var end_of_file:  boolean);
var
      cc:  char;
      c:   pseudo_char;
      j:   token_index;
begin
        if not end_of_file
           then begin
                    c := null;
                    while (class[c] = delimiter) and not eof (FILE)
                        do begin
                                read (FILE, cc);
                                c := ord(cc);
                            end;

                    if eof (FILE)
                       then end_of_file := true
                       else begin
                                j := 0;
                                repeat
                                    j := j + 1;
                                    token.c[j] := c;
                                    read (FILE, cc);
                                    c := ord(cc);
                                until (class[c]=delimiter) or eof (FILE);

                                token.length := j;
                            end;
                end;
end;
```

18.4.3   *output_token_to_disk_dictionary*

To output the token to the disk dictionary, we must add it to the disk block in the current buffer, if it will fit. If it will not fit, then the current block must be written to the disk dictionary file, and a new block started. Remember that we separate words by a null character.

```
procedure output_token_to_disk_dictionary (token: token_type);
var
        i:  token_index;
        search_token:  search_token_type;
begin
        translate_for_search (token, search_token);
        if next+search_token.length ≥ length_of_disk_block
          then output_disk_block;

        if next = 0
          then begin
                        n_disk_block := n_disk_block + 1;
                        disk_index[n_disk_block].first_word := search_token;
                end;
        disk_index[n_disk_block].last_word := search_token;

        for i := 1 to search_token.length
         do begin
                disk_buffer[current_buffer][next] := search_token.c[i];
                next := next + 1;
            end;
        disk_buffer[current_buffer][next] := 0;
        next := next + 1;
end;
```

To actually write a block to the disk,

```
procedure output_disk_block;
var
        i:  0..length_of_disk_block;
begin
        for i := next to length_of_disk_block
         do disk_buffer[current_buffer][i] := null;

        direct_write (n_disk_blocks, disk_buffer[current_buffer]);

        disk_buff_list[current_buffer].d_block_number := n_disk_blocks;

        current_buffer := 1 + current_buffer mod n_disk_buffers;
        next := 0;
end;
```

8.4.4   *finish_disk_dictionary_creation*

This is also exactly what is needed for the *finish_disk_dictionary_creation* procedure, followed by resetting the disk dictionary, master dictionary and modification file.

```
procedure finish_disk_dictionary_creation;
begin
        output_disk_block;
        reset (DICT);

        close (MASTER);
        close (MOD_IN);
        mod_file_has_changed := false;
end;
```

This finishes our work with local dictionaries. We have defined the procedures and data structures to allow user files to create and store lists of words which are local to a particular author or subject area.

9.0   User Control of the Speller

Several procedures remain to be designed which keep the user informed and in control of the execution of the speller.

9.1   *write_statistics*

There are two types of statistics that may be of interest:

(1) Statistics covering the properties of the file or files in this session.

(2) Statistics on the performance of the speller.

In the first category are statistics such as the following,

(1) number of characters read;

(2) number of tokens read;

(3) number of lines read;

(4) number of tokens not found in dictionary;

(5) number of tokens loaded from local dictionaries;

In the second category are,

(6) number of compare instructions;

(7) number of tokens found in list of common words;

(8) number of tokens found in hash table of document words;

(9) number of tokens found in disk dictionary;

(10) average hash chain length;

(11) number of incorrectly spelled candidates generated;

(12) number of times each procedure is called;

These latter statistics can be useful in finding the time–consuming parts of the speller, and tuning it to improve its performance.

To compute these statistics, we simply define a bunch of counters and increment them when appropriate. This requires spreading the increments around, and writing a procedure to print their values when requested. We define two sets of counters, counters for the current file (*nr*——) and for the entire session (*nt*——). The session counters merely accumulate the statistics for each file to provide cumulative statistics.

```
(* statistics counters *)

nr_lines:  counter;
nr_tokens:  counter;
nr_chars:  counter;

nr_found_1:  counter;
nr_found_2:  counter;
nr_found_3:  counter;
nr_not_found:  counter;
nr_compare:  counter;

nt_lines:  counter;
nt_tokens:  counter;
nt_chars:  counter;
```

```
nt_found_1:   counter;
nt_found_2:   counter;
nt_found_3:   counter;
nt_not_found:   counter;
nt_compare:   counter;


procedure write_statistics;
begin
      writeln (TTYO);
      write (TTYO, nr_chars:6,  ' characters read  ');,
      writeln (TTYO, '(' nt_chars:6, ')');
      write (TTYO, nr_tokens:6, ' tokens read       ');
      writeln (TTYO, '(', nt_tokens:6, ')');
      write (TTYO, nr_lines:6,  ' lines read        ');
      writeln (TTYO, '(', nt_lines:6, ')');

      writeln (TTYO);
      write (TTYO, n_hash_chain_entries:6, ' hash table entries    ');
      writeln (TTYO, '(', hash_chain_length:6, ' maximum)');
      write (TTYO, n_substitution_table:6, ' substitution table entries  ');
      writeln (TTYO, '(', max_substitution_table_length:6, ' maximum)');
      write (TTYO, n_inserted_word_buffer:6, ' inserted words ');
      writeln (TTYO, '(', max_inserted_words:6, ' maximum)');

      writeln (TTYO);
      write (TTYO, nr_found_1:6,   ' tokens found in graph      ');
      writeln (TTYO, '(', nt_found_1:6, ')');
      write (TTYO, nr_found_2:6,   ' tokens found in hash table ');
      writeln (TTYO, '(', nt_found_2:6, ')');
      write (TTYO, nr_found_3:6,   ' tokens found on disk       ');
      writeln (TTYO, '(', nt_found_3:6, ')');
      write (TTYO, nr_not_found:6, ' tokens not found           ');
      writeln (TTYO, '(', nt_not_found:6, ')');
      write (TTYO, nr_compare:6,   ' compares                   ');
      writeln (TTYO, '(', nt_compare:6, ')');

      writeln (TTYO);
      writeln (TTYO);
   end;
```

9.2   set_modes

We have mentioned that the user needs the ability to modify the operation of
the speller by setting various mode switches. The modes which we have used so far
are:

```
mode:  record
              quit:  boolean;
              skip:  boolean;

              number_check:  boolean;
              mixed_alphanumerics:  boolean;
              ignore_uppers:  boolean;

              correct:  boolean;

              end_of_file:  boolean;
       end;
```

We need a means of allowing the user to set these switches. Our *get_command* facility provides this function, and so we define a third table of commands, *table_3*, by,

```
table_3:   command_table;

procedure table_3_initialize;
begin
       table_3.prompt := "";
       table_3.next := null;

       enter_command_table (table_3, help, 'help ');
       enter_command_table (table_3, quit, 'exit ');
       enter_command_table (table_3, quit, 'quit ');
       enter_command_table (table_3, skip, 'skip ');
       enter_command_table (table_3, train, 'train ');
       enter_command_table (table_3, notrain, 'notrain ');
       enter_command_table (table_3, number, 'number ');
       enter_command_table (table_3, nonumber, 'nonumber ');
       enter_command_table (table_3, mixed, 'mixed ');
       enter_command_table (table_3, nomixed, 'nomixed ');
       enter_command_table (table_3, uppers, 'uppers ');
       enter_command_table (table_3, nouppers, 'nouppers ');
       enter_command_table (table_3, correct, 'correct ');
       enter_command_table (table_3, check, 'check ');
       enter_command_table (table_3, list, 'list ');
   end;
```

This leads to the following code to set our **mode switches,**

```
procedure set_modes;
var
       cmd:  command;
       complete:  boolean;
```

```
begin
      repeat
              complete := false;

              get_command (cmd, table_3);

              case cmd of   •

                     help:   list_commands (table_3);
                     quit:   complete := true;
                     skip:   mode.skip := true;
                     train:   mode.train := true;
                     notrain:   mode.train := false;
                     number:   mode.number_check := true;
                     nonumber:   mode.number_check := false;
                     mixed:   mode.mixed_alphanumerics := true;
                     nomixed:   mode.mixed_alphanumerics := false;
                     uppers:   mode.ignore_uppers := false;
                     nouppers:   mode.ignore_uppers := true;
                     correct:   mode.correct := true;
                     check:   mode.correct := false;
                     list:   list_modes;

              end (* case *);
      until complete;
end;
```

9.2.1   list_modes

The *list_modes* procedure is a minor formatting problem.

```
procedure list_modes;
begin
      writeln (TTYO);
      writeln (TTYO, 'Current Mode is:');
      writeln (TTYO);

      if mode.number_check
         then writeln (TTYO, 'Numbers are checked.');
      if mode.mixed_alphanumerics
         then writeln (TTYO, 'Mixed letters and numbers are checked.');
      if mode.ignore_uppers
         then writeln (TTYO, 'Strictly upper case words are not checked.');
```

```
      if mode.quit
         then writeln (TTYO, 'About to abort session')
      else if mode.skip
         then writeln (TTYO, 'About to skip to end-of-file')
      else if mode.correct
         then writeln (TTYO, 'Checking and correcting.')
         else writeln (TTYO, 'Checking for misspellings.');

      if mode.train
         then writeln (TTYO, '  Training mode.');

   end;
```

19.3   define_context

We also notice that our display context data structure and algorithm is so effectively parameterized by sizes of the upper, middle, and lower regions that this can be set by the user (within limits). This requires a new *table_1* command:

```
      enter_command_table (table_1, context, 'context ');
```

and an addition to the **case** statement in *obey_table_1_command*.

```
      context:   define_context;
```

The *define_context* procedure is then,

```
procedure define_context;
begin
      repeat (* until legal values *)

            repeat
                  write (TTYO, 'Size of upper region:  ');
                  readln (TTYI, n_upper);
            until n_upper ≥ 0;

            repeat
                  write (TTYO, 'Size of middle region:  ');
                  readln (TTYI, n_middle);
            until n_middle ≥ 0;

            repeat
                  write (TTYO, 'Size of lower region:  ');
                  readln (TTYI, n_lower);
            until n_lower ≥ 0;
```

```
              if n_upper+n_middle+n_lower > max_lines
                 then writeln (TTYO, 'Total context exceeds ',
                                          max_lines:4, ' lines.');

       until n_upper+n_middle+n_lower ≤ max_lines;

       if n_middle = 0
          then if n_lower > 0
                  then begin
                              n_lower := n_lower -1;
                              n_middle := 1;
                       end
          else if n_upper > 0
                  then begin
                              n_upper := n_upper -1;
                              n_middle := 1;
                       end;

       n_lines := n_upper+n_middle+n_lower;

       if n_lines = 0
          then begin_middle := 0
          else begin_middle := n_upper+1;

       end_middle := begin_middle + n_middle;
    end;
```

9.4   Skip and Train Modes

The *skip* and *train* modes were included in the *table_3* definition although we have yet to indicate how they are implemented.

The *skip* mode is set when the user no longer wants to check the remainder of the input file for correct spellings, but the rest of the input file should be copied directly to the output file. (This differs from *quit* mode which essentially aborts the speller.) To implement *skip* mode, we must add appropriate tests to bypass the spelling checking procedures. Several opportunities are available.

One possibility is to generate an automatic *accept* command in *check_for_generated_command*. This would cause the speller to accept all tokens which might be misspelled. However, note that although the user would see nothing, the speller would in fact be checking all tokens for correct spellings, and then ignoring the result of the dictionary search.

A better implementation is in *check_spelling* which can be modified to:

```
procedure check_spelling;
var
      token:  token_type;
begin
      per_file_initialize;

      repeat
               get_token (token);

               if not mode.skip
                  then begin

                             search_dictionary (token, found);

                                 if not found
                                    then ask_user_about_it (token);
                      end;

                 output_token (token);

             until mode.end_of_file or mode.quit;

             per_file_conclusion;
      end;
```

This implementation skips the entire checking mechanism, simply reading and writing tokens. However, note that we are still taking the time to determine what is and is not a token, even though the distinction is no longer relevant.

Still a third implementation would be to modify *find_non_delimiter* in *get_token*, as,

```
procedure find_non_delimiter (var c: char);
begin
      while ((class[c] = delimiter) or mode.skip) and (c ≠ end_of_file)
         do begin (* skip delimiters *)
                  put_output (c);
                  get_character_from_context_buffer (c);
             end;
end;
```

This implementation simply copies character by character from input to output with no interpretation whatsoever of the characters copied.

In choosing between these three implementations of the *skip* mode, we consider two things: performance and meaning. The performance is obviously best with *find_non_delimiter* and worse with *check_for_generated_spelling*. However, the intuitive meaning of the *skip* command is to skip checking tokens; it is still cast as a property of tokens. Therefore, even though modifying *find_non_delimiter* might produce a somewhat faster speller, we prefer to modify *check_spelling*, to try to match the semantics of our implementation with the semantics of the command.

Training mode is handled similarly. We want training mode to mean that each token which is unknown to the speller (not found in the dictionary) is in fact correct, and should be inserted into the local dictionary. The natural implementation is in *check_for_generated_command* which becomes,

```
procedure check_for_generated_command (var token: token_type;
                                        var complete: boolean);
var
    i: substitution_table_index;
    found: boolean;
begin
    complete := false;

    search_substitution_table (token, i, found);
    if found
        then begin
                complete := true;
                token := substitution_table[i].new;
            end;

    if not complete and mode.train
        then begin
                insert_token (token);
                complete := true;
            end;
end;
```

With these two new modes, we see how our basic program design structure allows easy modification. If new operating modes are needed for some environments, they should be as easy to add.

20.0   Memory Management

The major portion of our design is now complete; we have considered all major problems. Now if we look back at our design we see that a major portion of our design is concerned with the definition and support of the following abstract data types:

      command tables (*table_1, table_2, table_3*)
      context buffer (*context_buffer*)
      graph of common words (*graph*)
      hash table of document words (*hash_table* and *hash_chain*)
      index to disk dictionary (*disk_index*)
      list of candidate spellings (*candidate*)
      substitution table (*substitution_table*)
      list of inserted words (*inserted_word_buffer*)

So far, we have treated these data structures as simple arrays of data entries, but this may not be the most effective memory management approach. The first three data structures (command tables, context buffer, and common words graph) can be ignored. They are all static structures of (essentially) fixed size. Similarly, the list of candidate spellings can be kept quite small; more than four or five candidates would probably be more of a distraction for the user than an assistance.

The remaining data structures (hash table, disk index, substitution table and inserted word buffer), however, are (potentially) large dynamic structures. Care must be taken if we are to be able to run our speller on machines with limited memory. Thus, we consider the representation of these data structures more closely.

Each of these data structures is composed of tokens. Tokens are variable length strings. Thus, we are faced with needing to represent variable length lists of variable length strings. We can represent these strings by a fixed length array of characters, but this representation has two opposing limitations: the maximum length of a token and the average memory utilization. From studies such as the Brown Corpus, we know that the length of tokens in English varies, up to a maximum of 44 characters in length (for their study). However, we also know that the average word length for English is only about 8 characters. Thus, if we allocate fixed length arrays of 44 characters, we will be wasting over 80% of our available memory. We can improve our memory utilization by decreasing our maximum token length. By decreasing our maximum token length to 16, we still wasting about half our memory space, but we are now rejecting (as too long) over 1% of all input tokens. This is too high a rate, particularly when we would suspect that longer words are more likely to be misspelled.

For efficient memory utilization, we must therefore use a variable length representation for stored tokens. For this, we use a *string pool*. We create a large array of characters. Tokens are represented by a first character index and a length. When a token of n characters is to be stored, the next n characters are reserved and the token is copied into them.

This representation of tokens allows each token to use only as many characters as are needed for its length. Also, we can share the string pool among the different major data structures, avoiding situations where the substitution table is full, but the other data structures still have room to spare. Also, the memory requirements of the major data structures themselves are now considerably reduced, since they are now only pointers into the shared string pool. Therefore, we will simply allocate fixed-length arrays to represent our major data structures.

A few details remain to be worked out. First, what kind of "character" is to be stored in the string pool: *char*, *pseudo-char*, or *search_char*? The hash table and disk index store *search_char* while the substitution table and inserted word buffer store *pseudo_char*. The inserted word buffer can certainly be changed over to *search_char*, as can the *old* field of a substitution table entry. We are somewhat reluctant to convert the *new* field to *search_char*. The user may want to replace an incorrectly spelled token by a new string of characters which includes delimiters; this cannot be stored in a string of *search_char*. However, there are already limits to our substitution capability anyway. The user cannot replace a token with a new token which exceeds our maximum token length. Also we are attempting to provide a spelling checker, not a general purpose substitution program. Thus, we feel that changing the *new* field to *search_char* is not unreasonable.

With this change made, we can now define the string pool by,

string_pool_index = 0..*max_string_pool_length*;

string_pool: **array** [*string_pool_index*] **of** *search_char*;

and we define a *string* as,

string = **record**
                length: *token_length*;
                first_char: *string_pool_index*;
    end;

Now to allocate memory in the string pool, we consider the operations on each of the data structures:

> *substitution_table*: add new *old, new* pair.

> *disk_index*: delete old and define new index.

> *inserted_word_buffer*: (1) add new word and (2) delete entire structure.

> *hash_table*: (1) add new word and (2) delete entire structure.

Our difficulty is with the deletion of all entries in a data structure. We obviously want to be able to reuse this space. Hence, either we must design an instance of a general dynamic memory allocation algorithm (such as first-fit, best-fit, buddy, or some such), or we need to organize our use of the data structures to allow a simpler (and faster) memory allocation algorithm to be designed for this particular case (for example, a stack allocation algorithm).

Trying to avoid a general dynamic memory allocation algorithm, let us examine the use of our data structures.

The substitution table always grows and is searched linearly. Thus, we should start allocating memory to this data structure at one end of our string pool and simply let it grow.

When the inserted word buffer is deleted, the disk index is also, and vice–versa. Notice that no word can be inserted until it has not been found in the dictionary. Thus, the disk dictionary must have been searched and so the disk index is defined, and in place whenever a word is inserted. Further, the disk index is redefined only when the modification file has changed. This occurs only (1) initially and (2) when the inserted word buffer has filled and been merged with the modification file (leaving the inserted word buffer empty), and (3) when a *clear* command is executed (which deletes both the inserted word buffer and the modification file).

Further, since the hash table is only a cache for the disk, we may delete it when the others are deleted. If the hash table overflows, we would expect this to be a sign that memory is tight all over, and so the inserted word buffer should be merged with the modification file (on disk) to free additional memory.

Thus, we may allocate our string pool as shown in Figure 8.

This memory management approach requires changing several existing procedures and the creation of a few new ones. The major procedures are assignment operators, *define_low_string* and *define_high_string* which create a string, at either the low or high end of the string pool, from a *search_token*. These are,

```
procedure define_low_string (srch_tok: srch_tok_type; var s: string);
var
        i: token_index;
        k: str_pool_index;
begin
        if pool_bottom + srch_tok.length > pool_top
            then str_pool_overflow;

        s.length := srch_tok.length;
        s.first_char := pool_bottom;

        k := pool_bottom;
        for i := 1 to s.length
          do begin
                    k := k + 1;
                    str_pool[k] := srch_tok.c[i];
              end;

        pool_bottom := k;
    end;
```

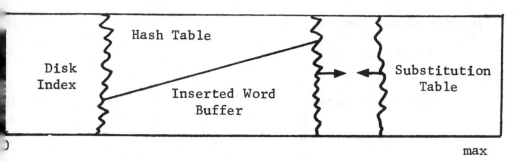

Figure 8. Allocation of memory in the string pool.

```
procedure define_high_string (srch_tok: srch_tok_type; var s: string);
var
        i: token_index;
        k: str_pool_index;
begin
        if pool_top - srch_tok.length < pool_bottom
           then str_pool_overflow;

        s.length := srch_tok.length;

        k := pool_top;
        i := s.length;
        while i > 0
           do begin
                        str_pool[k] := srch_tok.c[i];
                        k := k - 1;
                        i := i - 1;
                end;

        pool_top := k;
        s.first_char := pool_top;
end;
```

In case of overflow, the string pool is full and must be reset by flushing the inserted word buffer, emptying the hash table and resetting the disk index. We can ave the situation of overflow resulting from a full hash table with an empty inserted word buffer. In this case, we do not need to redefine the disk index.

```
procedure str_pool_overflow;
var
      i: hsh_tbl_index;
begin

      flush_new_word_buffer;

      (* delete all hash table entries *)

      for i := 0 to max_hsh_tbl
       do hsh_tbl[i] := null;

      n_hsh_chn_entries := 0;

      (* redefine disk index, if necessary *)
      if mod_file_has_changed
         then pool_bottom := 0
         else with dsk_index[n_dsk_blocks].last_word
               do pool_bottom := first_char + length;

end;
```

Finally, we need a few utility routines: (1) a *string_compare* procedure to compare a *search_token* with a string in the string table, to allow searching the hash table, inserted word buffer and substitution table; (2) a *write_mod_string* procedure to write strings from the inserted word buffer to the modification file; and (3) a *change_to_pseudo* procedure to convert the *new* string of an automatic substitution from *search_char* to *psuedo_char*. These are simple routines which we do not include here.

An obvious improvement on this design would be to design a more general memory management algorithm. However, there are many other improvements that can also be made. We list a few of them later.

21.0   Implementation

The completeness of our design allows easy implementation of a spelling program. This complete design document was produced and maintained in an on-line file system. This entire document (except for the figures) was produced using a text formatter and computer-driven photo-typesetter. The sections of code developed in this design are bracketed with *.code* and *.end_code* text formatting macro invocations. When the design was complete, the *.code* and *.end_code* formatting macros were redefined to delete all non-code portions of this document. This produced the raw code for our spelling program.

Once the raw code was isolated from the text of this design document, a massive text editing task was necessary. The code was in the wrong order for a Pascal compiler, and so several hours of text editing were necessary to rearrange the code to the form demanded by Pascal: constants, then types, then variables, and then procedures. *The order of procedure definition in our top-down design was exactly the wrong order for Pascal.* The top-down design produced higher level uses of procedures which were then defined; Pascal requires that each procedure be defined before it is used.

It was also necessary to reprogram much of the input/output of the speller. The *direct_read* and *direct_write* procedures were written to conform with the particular implementation available. Further, all interactive reads required a preceding *readln*. Both *TTYO* and *TTYI* were replaced by *TTY*.

A most annoying compiler limitation was the limitation of variable names to 10 characters. Variable names could exceed 10 characters, but only the first 10 are stored and used to distinguish between different variables. This was easily solved by massive substitution for variable names in the text editor, but destroyed some of the readability of the program.

Further problems arose with the use of a *set* value in the **case** statement in *check_class_of_token*. This required code to create an integer encoding of the set which was then used in the **case**.

Appropriate values for the program constants were decided upon. Most of these constants define the lengths of the several arrays used in the speller, and their values were determined by consideration of total available memory.

With these language and implementation dependent changes, the speller was then compiled and executed. It would be misleading to maintain that the program worked the first time; over 100 changes were necessary to produce a working program. However, most of these changes were minor syntactic problems. Since syntax checking did not occur during design, missing semicolons, unmatched ends, undeclared local variables, typing errors and so forth accounted for most of the errors. There were also some major debugging problems which were the result of variables not being properly initialized or parameters for which the keyword **var** was not declared. There were (surprisingly) no instances of design errors requiring coding changes.

Several limitations of the Pascal programming language became apparent during our implementation. The rigid order of text imposed by Pascal was quite annoying (because of its complete opposition to the top-down design). More importantly the lack of support for abstract data structures and clustering of procedures does not reflect the central role in our design of sets of procedures grouped with associated data structures.

Despite these problems, the program works as designed. Our complete program is presented in Appendix III. A *debug* mode has been added to allow the program to be traced. In addition each procedure calls an *enter_procedure* and an *leave_procedure* routine allowing performance statistics and traces to be produced if desired.

We intend to now translate this design into other programming languages, such as C and assembly language. This will allow the program to be executed on systems which do not support Pascal.

Translating the design to other languages will also help to improve the performance of the speller. Our current implementation appears to be somewhat sluggish. We expect that substantial improvements can be made in both the memory and time requirements of the speller by relatively simple optimizations of the existing program. This includes promoting some parameters to global variables (such as *token*, *search_token*, *found*, and so forth) to reduce the time for parameter passing and procedure entry/exit, and the macro substitution of procedures which are called exactly once in the entire program, such as the initialization routines, and many of the procedures called by *get_token*.

In addition other changes to our program (such as the form of the display for cursor–addressable CRTs) will also be made, all in the context of our existing design.

22.0   Improvements

Several points of improvement have been noted during the development and use of this speller. Most of these consist of minor changes in the user interface or algorithms to improve performance or convenience. Since these types of changes will continue to arise, and we need to define the end of this project somewhere, these improvements are left for other times and other programmers, as they feel necessary. We list below some of these improvements/modifications.

* The *edit* command was not defined. The major reason for this is that the design of the *edit* command should follow the design of the major text editor in use at each site. Since these vary greatly, we have chosen not to define this procedure. We would expect uses of this command to be rare and mainly for minor intra-line editing.

* If local dictionaries can be added to the disk dictionary by the *load* command, then there should be a *delete* or *remove* command which removes words from the disk dictionary. This might be used both to speed searching and to prevent words which are correct in general but not in this context from being thought correct by the speller.

* The need to explicitly exit from the *set_mode* sub-command procedure is annoying. An alternate command input algorithm allowing automatic transfer to and from mode setting when a command is given which is appropriate for the

different command tables might be easier for the user to handle. That is, if a mode setting command were given, it would automatically put the user in the mode setting procedure until a non–mode setting command were given, at which point the user would be put back in the non–mode setting procedure.

* Provision should be made with the current interactive question–answering mode of specifying parameters to allow any command to be cancelled by the user at any time. Thus, if a *load* command were incorrectly given, a special character could be used to cancel the command when the file name was requested.

* Line numbers can be added to the context display, for those systems whose text editors typically identify text by line numbers.

* A problem with the use of spelling programs for many computer science papers is the use of variable names and computer code. These symbols are often not correctly spelled words, and the user does not want to either *insert* them (since they are acceptable only in specific contexts) or *accept* each occurrence of them (there are too many occurrences). One syntax mode (*mode.ignore_uppers*) was partially motivated by the desire to ignore most of this type of text, which is often displayed in all upper case characters. However, some new languages, like Pascal, allow both upper and lower case characters to be used.

In many cases, special "markers" may exist which define the text to be ignored. These markers may be intrinsic to the languages (like parentheses in LISP or begin/end for block structured languages), formatting commands (*.code/.end_code* is used to format the code in this document), or font changes.

In view of the variety of markers used to define text which is to be ignored for purposes of spelling checking, the specific markers used must be specified by the user for each file. One general mechanism to allow this would be the definition of two *ignore* strings: *begin_ignore* and *end_ignore*. These strings could be null (feature not in use) or defined to match the specific markers for the file under consideration.

* Another step towards allowing users to modify the speller for their own situations occurs with the definition of what constitutes a token. Looking at our *get_token* procedure, we see that this is controlled by the *class* and *upper_or_lower* arrays. If the need should arise, there is no reason not to allow the user to redefine these arrays, within limits. The major side–effect is the definition of the characters sent to the *search_dictionary* routine and its *search_char* type definition, as computed from *search_code*.

* The correction algorithm can probably be speeded up by the use of a digram matrix. This can be added to the *try* procedures or to the *search_dictionary* procedure. The idea is to quickly filter out obviously incorrect tokens, avoiding a length dictionary search. Studies, such as the Brown Corpus, show that only about 25 percent of the possible letter pairs (digrams) actually occur in standard

English. Thus, if we construct (and maintain) a simple Boolean matrix $digram[i,j]$ which indicates whether letter i can be followed by letter j in any word in our dictionary, then we can use this matrix to avoid searching for many incorrect words. If any letter pair ($token.c[i]$, $token.c[i+1]$) is not in the $digram$ matrix, then we known that this token will not be found in a search of the dictionary. This is particularly important for the correction routines which may generate a large number of incorrect tokens trying to guess a correct spelling.

In fact, the number and position of incorrect digram pairs in a token can provide guidance on where the token is in error and if it can be corrected by our four rules. If a letter is missing, at most one digram can be wrong, and the missing letter must be between the incorrect digram. For a wrong letter or an extra letter, as many as two digrams could be wrong (but they must be adjacent). For a transposition, up to three (adjacent) digram errors are possible. Of course, there may not be any incorrect digrams, and we must proceed as currently, so the digram matrix is only a performance booster, and then only if it is sparse.

Notice that we need no more than one bit per digram entry to indicate whether that digram is or is not possible in some word in the dictionary. Thus, we have a binary digram matrix. A full digram matrix with the frequency of each entry might be of use in improving our guessing algorithm (guess that candidate with the largest sum or product of digram frequencies), but may cost much more in space. The simple binary digram matrix requires no more than 26 x 26 bits (less than 100 bytes) (plus the code to create, maintain and access it).

* Another modification aimed at improving performance is to use a limited batch search technique. Rather than search for each token as it is found, collect a list of all unique tokens in some quantity of text (call it a page). Then the dictionary is searched for each word in this list. The advantage of this search technique is that the larger the page size, the more times some tokens will occur. These multiple occurrence tokens will only need to be searched for (in the dictionary) once, thus reducing the time spent searching the dictionary. (Consider the extreme cases of a page being equal to an entire file, which is the typical batch mode speller, or the page being equal to only one token, which is the typical interactive speller.) A disadvantage is the reduced interactive nature of the speller. Also, identification, context display, and correction of misspelled tokens may be more difficult.

The advantages/disadvantages of this approach probably vary with the expected density of spelling errors. A higher density argues for a more interactive speller. This is further complicated, however, by the observation that files may often be run through the speller several times, with a large number of errors the first time, but only minor errors (due to changes) on subsequent runs.

23.0   Conclusions

There are undoubtedly many other improvements and modifications which can be suggested — no program can ever please everyone. However, we feel that the given design defines an extremely useful program. More importantly, the design is modular, well-structured, correct, easy to understand and may be easily modified to suit special needs.

Thus, we feel that the goals of this project have been met: we have designed a major program using a modern programming methodology, top-down design. We have shown that the methodology can work for real problems.

However, we have also learned several other things. Top-down design may produce many similar procedures, procedures which with enough foresight could be combined into one parameterized routine. The methodology also produces a large number of procedures which are used in exactly one place in the program, and although the program may work correctly, it may not work quickly.

We have also learned some things about the programming language Pascal. Pascal is not directly supportive of a top-down program, but rather of a bottom-up presentation. Further, the strong type checking (one of the advantages of Pascal) may in fact make reasonable memory management more difficult. Some desirable features (such as direct access files) are missing, and some implementations place undesirable restrictions on symbolic names.

We hope now to see this design refined and put to use by a large community of users.

Bibliography

1. C. N. Alberga, "String Similarity and Misspellings", *Communications of the ACM*, Volume 10, Number 5, (May 1967), pages 302–313.

    Master's Thesis. Reviews previous work. Mentions two researchers at IBM Watson who suggest finding the longest common substrings and assigning probabilities based on the portion of the correct string matched. Does rather extensive but unreadable analysis of different algorithms, but with no real results. Reviewed in *Computing Reviews*, Volume 8, Number 5, Review 12,712.

2. W. W. Bledsoe and I. Browning, "Pattern Recognition and Reading by Machine", *Proceedings of the Eastern Joint Computer Conference*, (1959), pages 225–232.

    Uses a small dictionary with probability of each word for OCR.

3. C. R. Blair, "A Program for Correcting Spelling Errors", *Information and Control*, Volume 3, Number 1, (March 1960), pages 60–67.

    Weights the letters to create a four or five letter abbreviation for each word. If abbreviations match, the words are assumed to be the same. Mentions the possibility (impossibility) of building in rules like: *i* before *e* except after *c* and when like *a* as in *neighbor* and *weigh*, ...

4. C. P. Bourne, "Frequency and Impact of Spelling Errors in Bibliographic Data Bases", *Information Processing and Management*, Volume 13, Number 1, (1977), pages 1–12.

    Examines the frequency of spelling errors in a sample drawn from 11 machine–readable bibliographic data bases. Finds that spelling errors are sufficiently severe that they should influence the search strategy to find information in the data base. Errors are not only in the input queries, but also in the data base itself.

5. G. Carlson, "Techniques for Replacing Characters that are Garbled on Input", *Proceedings of the 1966 Spring Joint Computer Conference*, (1966), pages 189–192.

    Uses trigrams to correct OCR input of genealogical records.

6. R. W. Cornew, "A Statistical Method of Spelling Correction", *Information and Control*, Volume 12, Number 2, (February 1968), pages 79–93.

    Uses digrams first, then a dictionary search to correct one character substitutions. Dictionary already exists for speech output problem.

7. F. J. Damerau, "A Technique for Computer Detection and Correction of Spelling Errors", *Communications of the ACM*, Volume 7, Number 3, (March 1964), pages 171–176.

    The four errors: wrong, missing, extra, transposed, are mentioned here as accounting for 80% of errors. Uses a bit vector for preliminary compare. (bit[i] is on if letter i is in word). Reviewed in *Computing Reviews*, Volume 5, Number 4, Review 5,962.

8. L. Davidson, "Retrieval of Misspelled Names in an Airlines Passenger Record System", *Communications of the ACM*, Volume 5, Number 3, (March 1962), pages 169–171.

    Abbreviates name to match stored name. Either name (token or dictionary) may be wrong.

9. E. G. Fisher, "The Use of Context in Character Recognition", COINS TR 76–12, Department of Computer and Information Sciences, University of Massachusetts, Amherst, (July 1976), 189 pages.

    Considers the problem of automatically reading addresses from letters by the Post Office; also Morse code recognition.

10. D. N. Freeman, *Error Correction in CORC: The Cornell Computing Language*, Ph.D. Thesis, Department of Computer Science, Cornell University, (September 1963).

11. E. J. Galli and H. M. Yamada, "An Automatic Dictionary and Verification of Machine-Readable Text", *IBM Systems Journal*, Volume 6, Number 3, (1967), page 192–207.

    Good discussion of the general problem of token identification and verification.

12. E. J. Galli and H. M. Yamada, "Experimental Studies in Computer–Assisted Correction of Unorthographic Text", *IEEE Transactions on Engineering Writing and Speech*, Volume EWS–11, Number 2, (August 1968), page 75–84.

Good review and explanation of techniques and problems.

13. J. J. Giangardella, J. Hudson and R. S. Roper, "Spelling Correction by Vector Representation Using a Digital Computer", *IEEE Transactions on Engineering Writing and Speech*, Volume EWS–10, Number 2, (December 1967), pages 57–62.

Defines hash functions to give a vector representation of a word as: Norm, Angle, and Distance. This speeds search time (over linear search) and aids in localizing the search for correct spellings since interchanged characters have the same Norm and extra or deleted letter is within fixed range.

14. H. T. Glantz, "On the Recognition of Information with a Digital Computer", *Journal of the ACM*, Volume 4, Number 2, (April 1957), pages 178–188.

Seems to want either exact match or greatest number of equal characters in equal positions. Good for OCR.

15. A. R. Hanson, E. M. Riseman and E. G. Fisher, "Context in Word Recognition", *Pattern Recognition*, Volume 8, Number 1, (January 1976), pages 35–45.

16. L. D. Harmon, "Automatic Reading of Cursive Script", *Proceedings of a Symposium on Optical Character Recognition*, Spartan Books, (January 1962), pages 151–152.

Uses digrams and a "confusion matrix" to give the probability of letter substitutions.

17. L. D. Harmon, "Automatic Recognition of Print and Script", *Proceedings of the IEEE*, Volume 60, Number 10, (October 1972), pages 1165–1176.

Surveys the techniques for computer input of print, including a section on error detection and correction. Indicates that digrams can catch 70 percent of incorrect letter errors.

18. E. B. James and D. P. Partridge, "Tolerance to Inaccuracy in Computer Programs", *Computer Journal*, Volume 19, Number 3, (August 1976), pages 207–212.

19. D. E. Knuth, *The Art of Computer Programming, Volume 3: Sorting and Searching*, Addison–Wesley, (1973), 722 pages.

20. H. Kucera and W. N. Francis, *Computational Analysis of Present–Day American English*, Brown University Press, (1967), 424 pages.

Gives frequency and statistical information for the Brown Corpus of over a million tokens.

21. L. A. Leslie, *20,000 Words*, McGraw–Hill, (1977), 282 pages.

Representative of several books which list words.

22. R. Lowrance and R. A. Wagner, "An Extension of the String-to-String Correction Problem", *Journal of the ACM*, Volume 22, Number 2, (April 1975), pages 175–183.

Extends Wagner and Fischer [1974] to include adjacent transpositions as an edit operation.

23. C. K. McElwain and M. E. Evans, "The Degarbler — A Program for Correcting Machine-Read Morse Code", *Information and Control*, Volume 5, Number 4, (December 1962), pages 368–384.

Uses digrams, trigrams and a dictionary to correct up to 70% of errors in machine recognized Morse code. Uses 5 special rules for the types of errors which can occur (dot interpreted as dash, ...)

24. L. E. McMahon, L. L. Cherry, and R. Morris, "Statistical Text Processing", *The Bell System Technical Journal*, Volume 57, Number 6, Part 2, (July–August 1978), pages 2137–2154.

Good description of how computer systems can be used to process text, including spelling correction and an attempt at a syntax checker.

25. H. L. Morgan, "Spelling Correction in Systems Programs", *Communications of the ACM*, Volume 13, Number 2, (February 1970), pages 90–94.

Use of spelling correction for compilers and operating system JCL. Uses dictionary with the four classes of errors. Also possible to use syntax and semantics to narrow search space. Reports on the CORC compiler [Freeman 1963] which associated a probability with each possible misspelling.

26. R. Morris and L. L. Cherry, "Computer Detection of Typographical Errors", *IEEE Transactions on Professional Communications*, Volume PC–18, Number 1, (March 1975), pages 54–64.

Describes the TYPO program for the UNIX system.

27.   F. Muth and A. L. Tharp, "Correcting Human Error in Alphanumeric
      Terminal Input", *Information Processing and Management*, Volume 13,
      Number 6, (1977), pages 329–337.

      Suggests a tree structure (like a trie) with special search procedures to
      allow corrections to be found. Damerau's review points out that their
      search strategies need improvement and that their tree is much too big to
      be practical. Each node of the tree has one character (data) and three
      pointers (father, brother, son). Reviewed in *Computing Reviews*, Volume
      19, Number 6, Review 33,119.

28.   J. A. O'Brien, "Computer Program for Automatic Spelling Correction",
      Technical Report RADC-TR-66-696, Rome Air Development Center,
      New York, (March 1967).

29.   T. Okuda, E. Tanaka and T. Kasai, "A Method for the Correction of
      Garbled Words Based on the Levenshtein Metric", *IEEE Transactions on
      Computers*, Volume C-25, Number 2, (February 1976), pages 172–177.

30.   D. P. Partridge and E. B. James, "Natural Information Processing", *Inter-
      national Journal of Man–Machine Studies*, Volume 6, Number 2, (March
      1974), pages 205–235.

      Uses a tree structure representation of words to allow checks for incorrect
      input words. Done in the context of correcting keywords in a Fortran
      program, but more is there. Frequencies are kept with tree branches to
      allow the tree to modify itself to optimize search.

31.   E. M. Riseman and R. W. Ehrich, "Contextual Word Recognition Using
      Binary Digrams", *IEEE Transactions on Computers*, Volume C-20,
      Number 4, (April 1971), pages 397–403.

      Indicates the important property of digrams is only their zero or non-zero
      nature.

32.   E. M. Riseman and A. R. Hanson, "A Contextual Postprocessing System
      for Error Correction Using Binary *n*-Grams", *IEEE Transactions on Com-
      puters*, Volume C-23, Number 5, (May 1974), pages 480–493.

      Suggests using digrams (2-grams), trigrams (3-grams), or in general
      n-grams, but only storing whether the probability is zero or non-zero (1
      bit). Also positional *n*-grams which keeps a separate *n*-gram table for
      each pair of positions (for each *i* and *j* we have the digram table for
      characters in position *i* and position *j* in a word).

33.   W. S. Rosenbaum and J. J. Hilliard, "Multifont OCR Postprocessing
      System", *IBM Journal of Research and Development*, Volume 19,
      Number 4, (July 1975), pages 398–421.

Very specific emphasis on OCR problems. Some on searching with a *match–any* character.

34. B. A. Sheil, "Median Split Trees: A Fast Look–up Technique for Frequently Occurring Keys", *Communications of the ACM*, Volume 21, Number 11, (November 1978), pages 947–958.

35. A. J. Szanser, "Error–Correcting Methods in Natural Language Processing", *Information Processing 68 – Proceedings of IFIP 68*, North Holland, Amsterdam, (August 1968), pages 1412–1416.

Confused paper dealing with correction for machine translation and automatic interpretation of shorthand transcript tapes. Suggests "elastic" matching.

36. A. J. Szanser, "Automatic Error–Correction in Natural Languages", *Information Storage and Retrieval*, Volume 5, Number 4, (February 1970), pages 169–174.

37. E. Tanaka and T. Kasai, "Correcting Method of Garbled Languages Using Ordered Key Letters", *Electronics and Communications in Japan*, Volume 55, Number 6, (1972), pages 127–133.

38. P. J. Tenczar and W. W. Golden, "Spelling, Word and Concept Recognition", Report CERL–X–35, University of Illinois, Urbana, Illinois, (October 1962).

39. R. B. Thomas and M. Kassler, "Character Recognition in Context", *Information and Control*, Volume 10, Number 1, (January 1967), pages 43–64.

Considers tetragrams (sequences of 4 letters). Of 27^4 possible tetragrams, only 12 percent (61,273) are legal.

40. L. Thorelli, "Automatic Correction of Errors in Text", *BIT*, Volume 2, Number 1, (1962), pages 45–62.

Sort of a survey/tutorial. Mentions digrams and dictionary look–up. Suggests maximizing probabilities.

41. C. M. Vossler and N. M. Branston, "The Use of Context for Correcting Garbled English Text", *Proceedings of the 19th ACM National Convention*, (August 1964), pages D2.4–1 to D2.4–13.

Uses confusion matrix and word probabilities to select the most probable input word. Also uses digrams. Trying to improve OCR input.

42. R. A. Wagner and M. J. Fischer, "The String–to–String Correction Problem", *Journal of the ACM*, Volume 21, Number 1, (January 1974), pages 168–173.

Algorithm for determining similarity of two strings as minimum number of edit operations to transform one into the other. Allowed edit operations are add, delete or substitute one character.

43. C. K. Wong and A. K. Chandra, "Bounds for the String Editing Problem", *Journal of the ACM*, Volume 23, Number 1, (January 1976), pages 13–16.

Shows that the complexity bounds of [Wagner and Fischer 1974] are not only sufficient but also necessary.

APPENDIX I

The 258 Most Common English Words

The following 258 words are the most commonly used words in written English text. They are derived from the most common words of the Brown Corpus [Kucera and Francis 1967], plus all those prefixes of these words which are legal words. We chose 258 for no particular reason except a desire to be able to check at least half the words in normal English text quickly by using our graph representation.

a	because	do	from
about	been	does	get
above	before	don't	give
after	began	down	go
again	being	each	going
air	below	earth	good
all	between	end	got
almost	big	enough	great
along	both	even	had
also	boy	ever	hand
always	boys	every	hard
an	but	eyes	has
and	by	far	have
animals	called	father	he
another	came	feet	head
any	can	few	help
are	children	find	her
around	come	first	here
as	could	following	high
asked	country	food	him
at	day	for	his
away	days	form	home
back	did	found	house
be	different	four	how

i	name	see	too
if	near	sentence	took
important	need	set	two
in	never	she	under
into	new	should	until
is	next	show	up
it	night	side	us
its	no	since	use
just	not	small	used
keep	now	so	very
kind	number	some	want
know	of	something	was
land	off	sometimes	water
large	often	soon	way
last	old	sound	we
left	on	still	well
let	once	story	went
life	one	study	were
light	only	such	what
like	or	take	when
line	other	tell	where
little	our	than	which
live	out	that	while
long	over	the	white
look	own	their	who
looked	page	them	why
made	paper	then	will
make	part	there	with
man	parts	these	without
many	people	they	word
may	picture	things	words
me	place	think	work
men	put	this	world
might	read	those	would
more	right	thought	write
most	said	three	year
mother	same	through	years
mr	saw	time	you
much	say	times	your
must	school	to	
my	second	together	

APPENDIX II

Definition of Common Word Graph

Using the 258 words of Appendix I, we construct the following graph for these words. The initial letter of the word is used as an index into the first 39 nodes of the graph. For each node of the graph, we list its index, the character for that node, whether or not this is a terminal node (by a space or apostrophe), and then the index of the next and alternate nodes.

As an example, the word "the" would index first to the node for "t" which would take us to node 313. At node 313, we need an "a" which does not match our "h" so we follow the alternate node to 315, then to 317 where we match our "h". Now our next node is 318, which needs an "a" which does not match our "e" so we take the alternate at 320 which matches our "e" and is an acceptable terminal node. Thus we have matched "the".

404 nodes

```
 0:[ a ',  40,    2]      0:[ q ,    0,    0]     46:[ a ,   47,    0]
 0:[ b ,   71,    3]      0:[ r ,  264,   19]     47:[ i ,  303,    0]
 0:[ c ,   91,    4]      0:[ s ,  267,   20]     48:[ i ,  404,   49]
 0:[ d ,  106,    5]      0:[ t ,  313,   21]     49:[ l ,   50,   57]
 0:[ e ,  119,    6]      0:[ u ,  351,   22]     50:[ l ',   0,   51]
 0:[ f ,  129,    7]      0:[ v ,  358,   23]     51:[ m ,   52,   53]
 0:[ g ,  148,    8]      0:[ w ,  360,   25]     52:[ o ,  219,    0]
 0:[ h ,  156,    9]      0:[ x ,    0,    0]     53:[ o ,  299,   54]
 0:[ i ', 171,   10]      0:[ y ,  398,    0]     54:[ s ,  350,   55]
 0:[ j ,  182,   11]      0:[ z ,    0,    0]     55:[ w ,   56,    0]
 0:[ k ,  183,   12]     40:[ b ,   41,   43]     56:[ a ,  107,    0]
 0:[ l ,  189,   13]     41:[ o ,   42,    0]     57:[ n ',  58,   64]
 0:[ m ,  207,   14]     42:[ u ,  386,  202]     58:[ d ',   0,   59]
 0:[ n ,  220,   15]     43:[ f ,   44,   45]     59:[ i ,   60,   63]
 0:[ o ,  234,   16]     44:[ t ', 364,    0]     60:[ m ,   61,    0]
 0:[ p ,  249,   18]     45:[ g ,   46,   48]     61:[ a ,   62,    0]
```

```
 62:[ l ', 401,   0]     110:[ f ,  111,   0]     158:[ n ,  393, 159]
 63:[ o ,  345, 378]     111:[ f ,  112,   0]     159:[ r ,  393, 160]
 64:[ r ,   65,  67]     112:[ e ,  113,   0]     160:[ s ',   0, 202]
 65:[ e ',   0,  66]     113:[ r ', 114,   0]     161:[ e ', 162, 164]
 66:[ o ,  304,   0]     114:[ e ,  178,   0]     162:[ a ,  393, 163]
 67:[ s ', 206,  68]     115:[ o ', 116,   0]     163:[ l ,  185, 372]
 68:[ t ',   0,  69]     116:[ e ', 401, 117]     164:[ i ,  165, 167]
 69:[ w ,   70,   0]     117:[ n ,  118, 248]     165:[ g ,  375, 166]
 70:[ a ,  378,   0]     118:[ ' ,  386,   0]     166:[ m ',   0, 401]
 71:[ a ,   72,  73]     119:[ a ,  120, 123]     167:[ o ,  168,   0]
 72:[ c ,  348,   0]     120:[ c ,  375, 121]     168:[ m ,  397, 169]
 73:[ e ',  74,  87]     121:[ r ', 122,   0]     169:[ u ,  170, 286]
 74:[ c ,   75,  77]     122:[ t ,  375,   0]     170:[ s ,  397,   0]
 75:[ a ,   76,   0]     123:[ n ,  124, 125]     171:[ f ',   0, 172]
 76:[ u ,  170,   0]     124:[ d ',   0, 336]     172:[ m ,  173, 179]
 77:[ e ', 303,  78]     125:[ v ,  126, 128]     173:[ p ', 174,   0]
 78:[ f ,   79,  80]     126:[ e ', 127,   0]     174:[ o ,  175,   0]
 79:[ o ,  372,   0]     127:[ n ',   0, 359]     175:[ r ,  176,   0]
 80:[ g ',  81,  82]     128:[ y ,  341,   0]     176:[ t ', 177,   0]
 81:[ a ,  303,   0]     129:[ a ,  130, 131]     177:[ a ,  178,   0]
 82:[ i ,  299,  83]     130:[ r ',   0, 345]     178:[ n ,  386,   0]
 83:[ l ,  188,  84]     131:[ e ,  132, 133]     179:[ n ', 180, 181]
 84:[ t ',  85,   0]     132:[ e ', 386, 286]     180:[ t ,  350,   0]
 85:[ w ,   86,   0]     133:[ i ,  134, 136]     181:[ s ',   0, 253]
 86:[ e ,  237,   0]     134:[ n ', 393, 135]     182:[ u ,  219,   0]
 87:[ i ,  300,  88]     135:[ r ', 219,   0]     183:[ e ,  184, 186]
 88:[ o ,   89,  90]     136:[ o ,  137, 145]     184:[ e ,  185,   0]
 89:[ t ,  375, 107]     137:[ l ,  138, 141]     185:[ p ',   0,   0]
 90:[ u ,  386, 378]     138:[ l ,  139,   0]     186:[ i ,  305, 187]
 91:[ a ,   92,  95]     139:[ o ,  140,   0]     187:[ n ,  188,   0]
 92:[ l ,   93,  94]     140:[ w ', 298,   0]     188:[ o ,  286,   0]
 93:[ l ', 357,   0]     141:[ o ,  393, 142]     189:[ a ,  190, 193]
 94:[ m ', 397, 303]     142:[ r ', 147, 143]     190:[ n ,  393, 191]
 95:[ h ,   96, 100]     143:[ u ,  144,   0]     191:[ r ,  192, 219]
 96:[ i ,   97,   0]     144:[ n ,  393, 404]     192:[ g ,  397,   0]
 97:[ l ,   98,   0]     145:[ r ,  146,   0]     193:[ e ,  194, 195]
 98:[ d ',  99,   0]     146:[ o ,  147,   0]     194:[ f ,  386, 386]
 99:[ r ,  237,   0]     147:[ m ',   0,   0]     195:[ i ,  196, 203]
100:[ o ,  101,   0]     148:[ e ,  386, 149]     196:[ f ,  397, 197]
101:[ m ,  397, 102]     149:[ i ,  202, 150]     197:[ g ,  333, 198]
102:[ u ,  103,   0]     150:[ o ', 151, 153]     198:[ k ,  397, 199]
103:[ l ,  393, 104]     151:[ i ,  299, 152]     199:[ n ,  397, 200]
104:[ n ,  105,   0]     152:[ o ,  393, 386]     200:[ t ', 201, 202]
105:[ t ', 359,   0]     153:[ r ,  154,   0]     201:[ t ,  257,   0]
106:[ a ,  107, 108]     154:[ e ,  155,   0]     202:[ v ,  397,   0]
107:[ y ', 401,   0]     155:[ a ,  386,   0]     203:[ o ,  204,   0]
108:[ i ,  109, 115]     156:[ a ,  157, 161]     204:[ n ,  300, 205]
109:[ d ',   0, 110]     157:[ d ',   0, 158]     205:[ o ,  206,   0]
```

```
206:[ k',  357,    0]      254:[ e ,  255,  258]      302:[ o ,  303,  304]
207:[ a ,  208,  211]      255:[ o ,  256,    0]      303:[ n',    0,    0]
208:[ d',  397,  209]      256:[ p ,  257,    0]      304:[ u ,  305,    0]
209:[ k ,  397,  210]      257:[ l ,  397,    0]      305:[ n',  393,    0]
210:[ n',  378,  378]      258:[ i ,  259,  262]      306:[ t ,  307,  311]
211:[ e',  303,  212]      259:[ c ,  260,    0]      307:[ i ,  316,  308]
212:[ i ,  332,  213]      260:[ t ,  261,    0]      308:[ o ,  359,  309]
213:[ o ,  214,  216]      261:[ u ,  372,    0]      309:[ u ,  310,    0]
214:[ r ,  397,  215]      262:[ l ,  263,  385]      310:[ d',  378,    0]
215:[ s ,  386,  345]      263:[ a ,  290,    0]      311:[ u ,  312,    0]
216:[ r',    0,  217]      264:[ e ,  265,  266]      312:[ c ,  375,    0]
217:[ u ,  218,  378]      265:[ a ,  393,    0]      313:[ a ,  314,  315]
218:[ c ,  375,  219]      266:[ i ,  332,    0]      314:[ k ,  397,    0]
219:[ s ,  386,    0]      267:[ a ,  268,  271]      315:[ e ,  316,  317]
220:[ a ,  221,  222]      268:[ i ,  393,  269]      316:[ l ,  381,    0]
221:[m ,  397,    0]      269:[m ,  397,  270]      317:[ h ,  318,  339]
222:[ e ,  223,  228]      270:[ w',    0,  378]      318:[ a ,  319,  320]
223:[ a ,  404,  224]      271:[ c ,  272,  275]      319:[ n',    0,  386]
224:[ e ,  393,  225]      272:[ h ,  273,    0]      320:[ e',  321,  326]
225:[ v ,  364,  226]      273:[ o ,  274,    0]      321:[ i ,  404,  322]
226:[ w',    0,  227]      274:[ o ,  381,    0]      322:[m',    0,  323]
227:[ x ,  386,    0]      275:[ e ,  276,  282]      323:[ n',    0,  324]
228:[ i ,  332,  229]      276:[ c',  277,  278]      324:[ r ,  397,  325]
229:[ o',  230,  231]      277:[ o ,  305,    0]      325:[ s ,  397,  378]
230:[ t',    0,  286]      278:[ e',    0,  279]      326:[ i ,  327,  329]
231:[ u ,  232,    0]      279:[ n ,  280,  386]      327:[ n',  328,  401]
232:[m ,  233,    0]      280:[ t',  281,    0]      328:[ g',  401,  348]
233:[ b',  364,    0]      281:[ e ,  289,    0]      329:[ o ,  330,  334]
234:[ f',  235,  238]      282:[ h ,  283,  287]      330:[ s ,  397,  331]
235:[ f',    0,  236]      283:[ e',    0,  284]      331:[ u',  332,    0]
236:[ t',  237,    0]      284:[ o ,  285,    0]      332:[ g',  333,    0]
237:[ e ,  303,    0]      285:[ u ,  392,  286]      333:[ h',  386,    0]
238:[ l ,  393,  239]      286:[ w',    0,    0]      334:[ r ,  335,    0]
239:[ n',  240,  243]      287:[ i ,  288,  291]      335:[ e ,  397,  336]
240:[ c ,  397,  241]      288:[ d ,  397,  289]      336:[ o ,  337,    0]
241:[ e',    0,  242]      289:[ n',  290,    0]      337:[ u ,  338,    0]
242:[ l ,  378,    0]      290:[ c ,  397,    0]      338:[ g ,  375,    0]
243:[ r',    0,  244]      291:[m ,  292,  293]      339:[ i ,  340,  342]
244:[ t ,  346,  245]      292:[ a ,  316,    0]      340:[m ,  341,    0]
245:[ u ,  246,  247]      293:[ o',  294,  306]      341:[ e',  401,    0]
246:[ r',    0,  386]      294:[m ,  295,  302]      342:[ o',  343,  349]
247:[ v ,  364,  248]      295:[ e',  296,    0]      343:[ g',  344,  347]
248:[ w ,  303,    0]      296:[ t ,  297,    0]      344:[ e ,  345,    0]
249:[ a ,  250,  254]      297:[ h ,  298,  301]      345:[ t',  346,    0]
250:[ g ,  397,  251]      298:[ i ,  299,    0]      346:[ h',  364,    0]
251:[ p ,  364,  252]      299:[ n ,  300,    0]      347:[ o',  348,    0]
252:[ r ,  253,    0]      300:[ g',    0,    0]      348:[ k',    0,    0]
253:[ t',  401,    0]      301:[ i ,  340,    0]      349:[ w ,  350,    0]
```

```
350:[ o ',    0,    0]        369:[ a , 386, 370]        388:[ r , 389, 391]
351:[ n , 352, 355]           370:[ e , 371, 373]        389:[ d ', 401, 390]
352:[ d , 364, 353]           371:[ n ',   0, 372]        390:[ k ',   0, 392]
353:[ t , 354,   0]           372:[ r ', 397,   0]        391:[ u , 392,   0]
354:[ i , 381,   0]           373:[ i , 374, 377]        392:[ l , 393,   0]
355:[ p ',    0, 356]         374:[ c , 375, 376]        393:[ d ',   0,   0]
356:[ s ', 357,   0]          375:[ h ',   0,   0]        394:[ r , 395,   0]
357:[ e ', 393,   0]          376:[ l , 397, 396]        395:[ i , 396,   0]
358:[ e , 359,   0]           377:[ o ',   0, 378]        396:[ t ', 397,   0]
359:[ r ', 378,   0]          378:[ y ',   0,   0]        397:[ e ',   0,   0]
360:[ a , 361, 365]           379:[ i , 380, 387]        398:[ e ', 399, 402]
361:[ n , 386, 362]           380:[ l , 381, 382]        399:[ a ', 400,   0]
362:[ s ',    0, 363]         381:[ l ',   0,   0]        400:[ r ', 401,   0]
363:[ t , 364, 378]           382:[ t ', 383,   0]        401:[ s ',   0,   0]
364:[ e , 404,   0]           383:[ h ', 384,   0]        402:[ o , 403,   0]
365:[ e ', 366, 368]          384:[ o , 385,   0]        403:[ u ', 404,   0]
366:[ l , 381, 367]           385:[ u , 386,   0]        404:[ r ',   0,   0]
367:[ n , 386, 372]           386:[ t ',   0,   0]
368:[ h , 369, 379]           387:[ o , 388, 394]
```

APPENDIX III

A Complete Spelling Program

The following is a complete, working spelling program developed from the design presented here. This program compiles and executes on a DECSystem-20 at the Laboratory for Computer Science at the Massachusetts Institute of Technology.

We begin by listing all procedure names.

1	direct_read	26	per_file_conclusion
2	direct_write	27	get_input
3	change_to_pseudo	28	put_output
4	translate_for_search	29	get_chr_from_input
5	write_token	30	put_chr_back_in_input
6	display_character	31	read_line
7	display_token	32	reset_regions
8	display_context	33	update_current_position
9	compare	34	get_char_from_context_buffer
10	srch_compare	35	put_char_back_in_context_buffer
11	string_compare	36	find_non_delimiter
12	enter_command_table	37	collect_possible_token
13	table_1_initialize	38	check_class_of_token
14	table_2_initialize	39	check_all_uppers
15	table_3_initialize	40	determine_if_token
16	init_common_words_graph	41	copy_to_delimiter
17	init_global_variables	42	get_token
18	list_commands	43	output_token
19	read_command	44	set_up_mod_files
20	srch_comad_table	45	put_mod_token
21	get_command	46	put_mod_string
22	get_input_file	47	reset_mod_files
23	get_output_file	48	get_next_from_file
24	init_variables_for_these_files	49	merge_with_modification_file
25	per_file_initialize	50	reverse_linked_list

51 flush_new_word_buffer
52 str_pool_overflow
53 define_low_string
54 define_high_string
55 set_up_for_disk_creation
56 get_next_merged_token
57 output_disk_block
58 put_token_to_disk_dictionary
59 finish_disk_dictionary_creation
60 define_disk_dictionary
61 srch_comon_words
62 hash
63 search_document_words
64 add_to_list_of_document_words
65 find_index_of_dsk_block
66 get_dsk_block
67 search_dsk_block
68 search_disk_dictionary
69 search_dictionary
70 insert_sorted
71 add_to_new_word_buffer
72 clear_new_word_buffer
73 clear_local_dictionary
74 dump_local_dictionary
75 collect_user_token
76 load_local_dictionary
77 new_cand
78 try_one_letter_wrong_at

79 try_transposed_letters
80 try_extra_letter
81 try_wrong_letter
82 try_missing_letter
83 display_guess
84 guess_correct_spelling
85 find_cands
86 list_modes
87 set_modes
88 define_context
89 write_statistics
90 insert_token
91 edit_context
92 list_cands
93 replace_with_cand
94 read_new_token
95 replace_token
96 remember
97 substitute_token
98 search_subst_tbl
99 check_for_generated_command
100 do_table_2_command
101 ask_user_about_it
102 check_spelling
103 execute_table_1_command
104 do_speller_directive
105 main_program

program SPELL;

```
(* ———————————————————————————————————— *)
(*                                                          *)
(*                                                          *)
(*           Constant Declarations                          *)
(*                                                          *)
(*                                                          *)
(* ———————————————————————————————————— *)
```

const
        null = 0;
        end_of_line = 128;
        end_of_file = 129;

        max_command_table_entries = 50;

        max_token_length = 40;

        max_lines = 30;

        max_line_length = 80;

        max_number_of_nodes = 420;

        max_hsh_tbl = 127;

        max_hsh_chn = 4000;

        length_of_dsk_block = 255;
        max_dsk_blocks = 1500;

        n_dsk_buffers = 4;

        max_cand_list_length = 8;

        max_subst_tbl = 100;

        max_new_word = 1000;

        max_str_pool = 50000;

        max_proc_number = 105;
        max_proc_level = 15;

```
(* _____ *)
(*                                                          *)
(*                                                          *)
(*            Type Declarations                             *)
(*                                                          *)
(*                                                          *)
(* _____ *)
```

type

        compare_result = (*less, equal, greater*);

        filename = *packed* **array** [1..20] **of** *char*;

```
(* - - - - - - - - - - - - - - - - - - - - - - - - - - - - *)
```

        command_string = *packed* **array** [1..11] **of** *char*;

        command = 0..*max_command_table_entries*;
        cmd_pool_index = 0..*max_command_table_entries*;

        command_table = **record**
                                prompt: *char*;
                                next: *cmd_pool_index*;
                        end;

```
(* - - - - - - - - - - - - - - - - - - - - - - - - - - - - *)
```

        pseudo_char = 0..130;
        search_char = 0..39;

        char_class = (*alphabetic, numeric, delimiter, apostrophe*);

```
(* - - - - - - - - - - - - - - - - - - - - - - - - - - - - *)
```

        token_length = 0..*max_token_length*;
        token_index = 0..*max_token_length*;

        token_type = **record**
                                length: *token_length*;
                                c: *packed* **array** [*token_index*] **of** *pseudo_char*;
                        end;

        srch_tok_type = **record**
                                length: *token_length*;
                                c: *packed* **array** [*token_index*] **of** *search_char*;
                        end;

```
(* - - - - - - - - - - - - - - - - - - - - - - - - - - - - - - *)

      line_index = 0..81 (* max_line_length + 1 *);

      line = record
                    length:  line_index;
                    c:  array [line_index] of pseudo_char;
             end;

      line_number = 0..max_lines;

(* - - - - - - - - - - - - - - - - - - - - - - - - - - - - - - *)

      node_index = 0..max_number_of_nodes;

      node = record
                    c:  search_char;
                    end_of_word:  boolean;
                    next:  node_index;
                    alt:  node_index;
             end;

(* - - - - - - - - - - - - - - - - - - - - - - - - - - - - - - *)

      hsh_tbl_index = 0..max_hsh_tbl;
      hsh_chn_index = 0..max_hsh_chn;

(* - - - - - - - - - - - - - - - - - - - - - - - - - - - - - - *)

      dsk_block = array [0..length_of_dsk_block] of search_char;
      dsk_block_index = 0..max_dsk_blocks;

      dsk_buff_index = 0..n_dsk_buffers;

(* - - - - - - - - - - - - - - - - - - - - - - - - - - - - - - *)

      cand_table_index = 0..max_cand_list_length;

(* - - - - - - - - - - - - - - - - - - - - - - - - - - - - - - *)

      subst_tbl_index = 0..max_subst_tbl;

(* - - - - - - - - - - - - - - - - - - - - - - - - - - - - - - *)

      new_word_index =  0..max_new_word;

(* - - - - - - - - - - - - - - - - - - - - - - - - - - - - - - *)
```

```
        counter = 0..99999999;
```

(* - *)

```
        str_pool_index = 0..max_str_pool;

        string = record
                          length:  token_length;
                          first_char:  str_pool_index;
                  end;
```

(* - *)

```
        proc_number = 0..max_proc_number;
        proc_string = packed array [1..32] of char;
```

(* —— *)
(*   *)
(*   *)
(*   Variable Declarations   *)
(*   *)
(*   *)
(* —— *)

var

```
        MOD_IN:  text;
        MOD_OUT:  text;
        USER:  text;
        MASTER:  text;
        DICT:  file of dsk_block;
```

(* - *)

```
        lower_case:  array [pseudo_char] of pseudo_char;

        bit:  array [char_class] of 1..4;

        class:  array [pseudo_char] of char_class;
        upper_or_lower:  array [pseudo_char] of (upper, lower, neither);

        search_code:  array [pseudo_char] of search_char;
        pseudo_code:  array [search_char] of pseudo_char;
```

(* - *)

```
display_form: array [pseudo_char]
                    of record
                                length: 0..2;
                                representation: array [1..2] of char;
                    end;
```

(* - *)

```
mode: record
                quit: boolean;
                skip: boolean;

                number_check: boolean;
                mixed_alphanumerics: boolean;
                ignore_uppers: boolean;

                correct: boolean;
                train: boolean;
                end_of_file: boolean;

                debug: 0..max_proc_level;
        end;
```

(* - *)

```
n_cmd_pool_entries: cmd_pool_index;
cmd_pool: array [cmd_pool_index]
                of record
                            number: command;
                            word: token_type;
                            next: cmd_pool_index;
                end;

table_1: command_table;
table_2: command_table;
table_3: command_table;
```

(* - *)

```
context_buffer: array [line_number] of line;

current_position: record
                            line: line_number;
                            column: line_index;
                    end;

context_is_displayed: boolean;
```

```
(* - - - - - - - - - - - - - - - - - - - - - - - - - - - - - - - - *)


    char_saved:  boolean;
    saved_character:  pseudo_char;

(* - - - - - - - - - - - - - - - - - - - - - - - - - - - - - - - - *)


    graph:  array [node_index] of node;

(* - - - - - - - - - - - - - - - - - - - - - - - - - - - - - - - - *)


    str_pool:  packed array [str_pool_index] of search_char;
    pool_bottom:  str_pool_index;
    pool_top:  str_pool_index;

(* - - - - - - - - - - - - - - - - - - - - - - - - - - - - - - - - *)


    hsh_tbl:  array [hsh_tbl_index] of hsh_chn_index;

    n_hsh_chn_entries:  hsh_chn_index;
    hsh_chn:  array [hsh_chn_index]
                  of record
                          word:  string;
                          link:  hsh_chn_index;
                  end;

(* - - - - - - - - - - - - - - - - - - - - - - - - - - - - - - - - *)


    n_dsk_blocks:  dsk_block_index;
    dsk_index:  array [1..max_dsk_blocks]
                  of record
                          first_word:  string;
                          last_word:  string;
                  end;

(* - - - - - - - - - - - - - - - - - - - - - - - - - - - - - - - - *)


    dsk_buffer:  array [1..n_dsk_buffers] of dsk_block;


    dsk_buff_list:  array [dsk_buff_index]
                      of record
                              d_block_number:  dsk_block_index;
                              forword:  dsk_buff_index;
                              backward:  dsk_buff_index;
                      end;

(* - - - - - - - - - - - - - - - - - - - - - - - - - - - - - - - - *)
```

```
    n_cands:  cand_table_index;
    cand:  array [cand_table_index] of token_type;

    guess_index:  cand_table_index;

(* - - - - - - - - - - - - - - - - - - - - - - - - - - - - - - *)

    n_subst_tbl:  subst_tbl_index;
    subst_tbl:  array [subst_tbl_index]
                   of record
                            old:  string;
                            new:  string;
                     end;

(* - - - - - - - - - - - - - - - - - - - - - - - - - - - - *)

    mod_file:  array [1..2] of filename;

    current_mod_file:  0..2;
    mod_file_has_changed:  boolean;

    end_of_mod_file:  boolean;
    end_of_master_file:  boolean;

    mod_token:  srch_tok_type;
    master_token:  srch_tok_type;

    current_buffer:  dsk_buff_index;
    next_in_buffer:  0..length_of_dsk_block;
    last_token:  srch_tok_type;

(* - - - - - - - - - - - - - - - - - - - - - - - - - - - - - - *)

    n_new_word:  new_word_index;
    new_word_buffer:  array [new_word_index]
                         of record
                                  link:  new_word_index;
                                  word:  string;
                           end;

(* - - - - - - - - - - - - - - - - - - - - - - - - - - - - - *)

    n_lines:  line_number;

    n_upper:  line_number;
    n_middle:  line_number;
    n_lower:  line_number;
```

```
        begin_middle:  line_number;
        end_middle:  line_number;
```

(* _ - *)

```
        nr_lines:  counter;
        nr_tokens:  counter;
        nr_chars:  counter;

        nr_found_1:  counter;
        nr_found_2:  counter;
        nr_found_3:  counter;
        nr_not_found:  counter;
        nr_compare:  counter;

        nt_lines:  counter;
        nt_tokens:  counter;
        nt_chars:  counter;

        nt_found_1:  counter;
        nt_found_2:  counter;
        nt_found_3:  counter;
        nt_not_found:  counter;
        nt_compare:  counter;
```

(* _ - - - - *)

```
        proc_level:  0..max_proc_level;
        proc_stack:  array [0..max_proc_level] of proc_number;

        proc_name:  array [proc_number] of proc_string;
        proc_depth:  array [proc_number] of 0..max_proc_level;
        proc_i_calls:  array [proc_number] of counter;
        proc_ij_calls:  array [proc_number]
                           of array [proc_number] of counter;
```

(* ——— *)
(* *)
(* *)
(*   Utility Procedures   *)
(* *)
(* *)
(* ——— *)

```
procedure enter_proc (i:  proc_number; s:  proc_string);
var
        j:  proc_number;
        k:  0..32;
```

```
begin
      proc_level := proc_level + 1;
      proc_stack[proc_level] := i;

      proc_i_calls[i] := proc_i_calls[i] + 1;
      if proc_i_calls[i] = 1
         then proc_name[i] := s;
      if proc_level > proc_depth[i]
         then proc_depth[i] := proc_level;


      if proc_level > 1
         then begin
                      j := proc_stack[proc_level-1];
                      proc_ij_calls[i][j] := proc_ij_calls[i][j] + 1;
              end;


      if mode.debug > proc_level
         then begin
                      for k := 1 to proc_level
                       do write (TTY, '   ');

                      k := 0;
                      repeat
                             k := k + 1;
                             write (TTY, s[k]);
                      until s[k] = ' ';
                      writeln (TTY);
              end;


end;

procedure leave_proc (i:  proc_number; s:  proc_string);
begin
      proc_level := proc_level - 1;
end;

(* * * * * * * * * * * * * * * * * * * * * * * * * * * * * * * * * * *)

procedure direct_read (j:  dsk_block_index; var b:  dsk_block);
begin
      enter_proc (  1,'direct_read                    ');
      setpos (DICT, j * (1+length_of_dsk_block));
      b := DICT^;
      leave_proc (  1,'direct_read                    ');
end;
```

```
procedure direct_write (j: dsk_block_index; b: dsk_block);
begin
        enter_proc (   2,'direct_write                           ');
        setpos (DICT, j * (1+length_of_dsk_block));
        DICT^ := b;
        put (DICT);
        leave_proc (   2,'direct_write                           ');
end;
```

(* *)

```
procedure change_to_pseudo (s:  string; var token:  token_type);
var
        i:   token_index;
        k:   str_pool_index;
begin
        enter_proc (   3,'change_to_pseudo                      ');
        k := s.first_char;
        for i := 1 to s.length
          do begin
                    k := k + 1;
                    token.c[i] := pseudo_code[str_pool[k]];
              end;
        token.length := s.length;

        leave_proc (   3,'change_to_pseudo                      ');
end;
```

(* *)

```
procedure translate_for_search (token:  token_type;
                                 var srch_tok:  srch_tok_type);
var
        i:  token_index;
        reject:  boolean;
begin
        enter_proc (   4,'translate_for_search                  ');
        reject := false;
        i := token.length;

        while (i > 0) and not reject
            do begin
                    srch_tok.c[i] := search_code[token.c[i]];
                    if srch_tok.c[i] = 0 then reject := true;
                    i := i - 1;
              end;
```

```
        if reject
           then srch_tok.length := 0
           else srch_tok.length := token.length;
        leave_proc (  4,'translate_for_search              ');
   end;
```

(* *)

```
procedure write_token (token:  token_type);
var
        j:  token_index;
begin
        enter_proc (  5,'write_token                      ');
        for j := 1 to token.length
          do write (TTY, chr(token.c[j]));
        leave_proc (  5,'write_token                     ');
   end;
```

(* *)

```
procedure display_character (c:  pseudo_char);
var
        k:  0..2;
begin
        enter_proc (  6,'display_character                ');
        if c = end_of_line
           then writeln (TTY)
           else for k := 1 to display_form[c].length
                   do write (TTY, display_form[c].representation[k]);
        leave_proc (  6,'display_character               ');
   end;
```

(* *)

```
procedure display_token (token:  token_type);
var
        j:  token_index;
begin
        enter_proc (  7,'display_token                    ');
        for j := 1 to token.length
          do display_character (token.c[j]);
        leave_proc (  7,'display_token                   ');
   end;
```

* *)

```
procedure display_context;
var
      i:   line_number;
      j:   line_index;
begin
      enter_proc (  8,'display_context                        ');
      if not context_is_displayed
         then for i := 1 to n_lines
                  do begin
                            for j := 1 to context_buffer[i].length
                              do display_character (context_buffer[i].c[j]);
                                   j := context_buffer[i].length;
                              if context_buffer[i].c[j] ≠ end_of_line
                                 then writeln (TTY);
                  end;

      context_is_displayed := true;

      leave_proc (  8,'display_context                        ');
end;
```

(* *)

```
procedure compare (t1:  token_type;
                   var result:  compare_result;
                   t2:  token_type;
                   var prefix:  boolean);
var
      j1:  token_index;
      n:   token_length;
begin
      enter_proc (  9,'compare                        ');
      prefix := false;

      if t1.length < t2.length
         then n := t1.length
         else n := t2.length;

      j1 := 0;
      repeat
            j1 := j1 + 1;
      until (j1≥n) or (t1.c[j1] ≠ t2.c[j1]);

      if t1.c[j1] < t2.c[j1]
         then result := less
         else if t1.c[j1] > t2.c[j1]
                 then result := greater
                 else begin
```

```
                          if t1.length < t2.length
                             then result := less
                             else if t1.length > t2.length
                                     then result := greater
                                     else result := equal;

                          prefix := (j1=t1.length);
                 end;

    nr_compare := nr_compare + 1;
    nt_compare := nt_compare + 1;
    leave_proc (  9,'compare                           ');
end;

* * * * * * * * * * * * * * * * * * * * * * * * * * * * * * * * *)

procedure srch_compare (t1:  srch_tok_type;
                        var result:  compare_result;
                        t2:  srch_tok_type);
var
    j1:  token_index;
    n:  token_length;
begin
    enter_proc ( 10,'srch_compare                     ');

    if t1.length < t2.length
       then n := t1.length
       else n := t2.length;

    j1 := 0;
    repeat
          j1 := j1 + 1;
    until (j1≥n) or (t1.c[j1] ≠ t2.c[j1]);

    if t1.c[j1] < t2.c[j1]
       then result := less
       else if t1.c[j1] > t2.c[j1]
               then result := greater
               else begin
                         if t1.length < t2.length
                            then result := less
                            else if t1.length > t2.length
                                    then result := greater
                                    else result := equal;
                  end;

    nr_compare := nr_compare + 1;
    nt_compare := nt_compare + 1;
    leave_proc ( 10,'srch_compare                     ');
end;
```

```
(* * * * * * * * * * * * * * * * * * * * * * * * * * * * * * * * * *)


procedure string_compare (t1:  srch_tok_type;
                          var result:  compare_result;
                          s:  string);
var
     j1:  token_index;
     j2:  str_pool_index;
     n:  token_length;
begin
     enter_proc ( 11,'string_compare                    ');

     if t1.length < s.length
        then n := t1.length
        else n := s.length;

     j1 := 0;
     j2 := s.first_char;
     repeat
          j1 := j1 + 1;
          j2 := j2 + 1;
     until (j1≥n) or (t1.c[j1] ≠ str_pool[j2]);

     if t1.c[j1] < str_pool[j2]
        then result := less
        else if t1.c[j1] > str_pool[j2]
                then result := greater
                else begin
                          if t1.length < s.length
                             then result := less
                             else if t1.length > s.length
                                     then result := greater
                                     else result := equal;
                end;

     nr_compare := nr_compare + 1;
     nt_compare := nt_compare + 1;
     leave_proc ( 11,'string_compare                    ');
end;

(* _____ *)
(*                                                          *)
(*                                                          *)
(*          Initialization                                  *)
(*                                                          *)
(*                                                          *)
(* _____ *)
```

```
procedure enter_command_table (var table:  command_table;
                               n:  command;
                               s:  command_string);
var
     p:  cmd_pool_index;
     j:  token_index;
begin
     enter_proc ( 12,'enter_command_table              ');
     (* get new pool entry *)
     n_cmd_pool_entries := n_cmd_pool_entries + 1;
     p := n_cmd_pool_entries;

     j := 0;
     repeat
           j := j + 1;
           cmd_pool[p].word.c[j] := lower_case[ord(s[j])];
     until (s[j+1] = ' ');
     cmd_pool[p].word.length := j;

     cmd_pool[p].number := n;

     (* link into command table *)
     cmd_pool[p].next := table.next;
     table.next := p;
     leave_proc ( 12,'enter_command_table              ');
end;


* * * * * * * * * * * * * * * * * * * * * * * * * * * * * * * * * * * * *)


procedure table_1_initialize;
begin
     enter_proc ( 13,'table_1_initialize              ');
     table_1.prompt := '*';
     table_1.next := null;

     enter_command_table (table_1, 1, 'help       ');
     enter_command_table (table_1, 2, 'quit       ');
     enter_command_table (table_1, 2, 'exit       ');
     enter_command_table (table_1, 2, 'end        ');
     enter_command_table (table_1, 3, 'check      ');
     enter_command_table (table_1, 4, 'correct    ');
     enter_command_table (table_1, 5, 'clear      ');
     enter_command_table (table_1, 6, 'load       ');
     enter_command_table (table_1, 7, 'dump       ');
     enter_command_table (table_1, 8, 'mode       ');
     enter_command_table (table_1, 9, 'statistics ');
     enter_command_table (table_1,10, 'context    ');
     leave_proc ( 13,'table_1_initialize              ');
end;
```

```
(* * * * * * * * * * * * * * * * * * * * * * * * * * * * * * * * * * * * * *)


procedure table_2_initialize;
begin
      enter_proc ( 14,'table_2_initialize                    ');
      table_2.prompt := '?';
      table_2.next := null;

      enter_command_table (table_2, 1, 'help          ');
      enter_command_table (table_2, 2, 'quit          ');
      enter_command_table (table_2, 2, 'exit          ');
      enter_command_table (table_2, 2, 'end           ');
      enter_command_table (table_2, 3, 'skip          ');
      enter_command_table (table_2, 4, 'accept        ');
      enter_command_table (table_2, 5, 'insert        ');
      enter_command_table (table_2, 6, 'replace       ');
      enter_command_table (table_2, 7, 'substitute ');
      enter_command_table (table_2, 8, 'edit          ');
      enter_command_table (table_2, 9, 'clear         ');
      enter_command_table (table_2,10, 'load          ');
      enter_command_table (table_2,11, 'dump          ');
      enter_command_table (table_2,12, 'mode          ');
      enter_command_table (table_2,13, 'display       ');
      enter_command_table (table_2,14, 'correct       ');
      enter_command_table (table_2,15, 'list          ');
      enter_command_table (table_2,16, 'statistics ');
      leave_proc ( 14,'table_2_initialize                   ');
end;

(* * * * * * * * * * * * * * * * * * * * * * * * * * * * * * * * * * * * * *)


procedure table_3_initialize;
begin
      enter_proc ( 15,'table_3_initialize                   ');
      table_3.prompt := '';
      table_3.next := null;

      enter_command_table (table_3, 1, 'help          ');
      enter_command_table (table_3, 2, 'exit          ');
      enter_command_table (table_3, 2, 'end           ');
      enter_command_table (table_3, 2, 'quit          ');
      enter_command_table (table_3, 3, 'skip          ');
      enter_command_table (table_3, 4, 'train         ');
      enter_command_table (table_3, 5, 'notrain       ');
      enter_command_table (table_3, 6, 'number        ');
      enter_command_table (table_3, 7, 'nonumber      ');
      enter_command_table (table_3, 8, 'mixed         ');
      enter_command_table (table_3, 9, 'nomixed       ');
```

```
      enter_command_table (table_3,10, 'uppers      ');
      enter_command_table (table_3,11, 'nouppers    ');
      enter_command_table (table_3,12, 'correct     ');
      enter_command_table (table_3,13, 'check       ');
      enter_command_table (table_3,14, 'list        ');
      enter_command_table (table_3,15, 'debug       ');
      leave_proc ( 15,'table_3_initialize            ');
end;

(* * * * * * * * * * * * * * * * * * * * * * * * * * * * * * * * * *)

procedure init_common_words_graph;
var
      i:    node_index;
      c:    char;

      skip:  char; (* for skipping over formatting characters *)
begin
      enter_proc ( 16,'init_common_words_graph           ');
      for i := 0 to max_number_of_nodes
       do with graph[i]
            do begin
                      c := null;
                      end_of_word := false;
                      next := null;
                      alt := null;
             end;

      reset (INPUT, 'COMMON.GPH');

      readln (INPUT, i) (* number of links *);

      while not eof(INPUT)
        do begin
                  read (INPUT, i);
                  read (INPUT, skip); (* : *)
                  read (INPUT, skip); (* [ *)
                  read (INPUT, c);

                  if i = 0
                     then i := search_code[ord(c)];
                  graph[i].c := search_code[ord(c)];

                  read (INPUT, c);
                  if c = ''''
                     then graph[i].end_of_word := true;
```

```
                        read (INPUT, skip); (* , *)
                        read (INPUT, graph[i].next);
                        read (INPUT, skip); (* , *)
                        read (INPUT, graph[i].alt);
                        readln (INPUT);
                end;

        close (INPUT);
        leave_proc ( 16,'init_common_words_graph          ');
end;
```

(* *)

```
procedure init_global_variables;
var
        c:  pseudo_char;
        i1:  proc_number;
        i2:  proc_number;
        i3:  line_number;
        i4:  hsh_tbl_index;
        i5:  dsk_buff_index;
begin

        proc_level := 0;
        for i1 := 0 to max_proc_number
          do begin
                        proc_i_calls[i1] := 0;
                        proc_depth[i1] := 0;
                        for i2 := 0 to max_proc_number
                          do proc_ij_calls[i1][i2] := 0;
                end;
        enter_proc ( 17,'init_global_variables          ');


        for c := 0 to 130
          do lower_case[c] := c;
        for c := ord('A') to ord('Z')
          do lower_case[c] := c - ord('A') + ord('a') ;

        bit[alphabetic] := 1; bit[numeric] := 2; bit[apostrophe] := 4;

        for c := 0 to 130 do class[c] := delimiter;
        for c := ord('0') to ord('9') do class[c] := numeric;
        for c := ord('A')to ord('Z') do class[c] := alphabetic;
        for c := ord('a')to ord('z') do class[c] := alphabetic;
        class[ord('''')] := apostrophe;
```

```
for c := 0 to 130 do upper_or_lower[c] := neither;
for c := ord('A')to ord('Z') do upper_or_lower[c] := upper;
for c := ord('a')to ord('z') do upper_or_lower[c] := lower;

for c := 0 to 130 do search_code[c] := 0;
for c := ord('a') to ord('z') do search_code[c] := c - ord('a') + 1;
for c := ord('A') to ord('Z') do search_code[c] := c - ord('A') + 1;
search_code[ord('''')] := 27;
for c := ord('0') to ord('9') do search_code[c] := c - ord('0') + 28;

for c := 0 to 130
  do if search_code[c] ≠ 0
       then pseudo_code[search_code[c]] := c;


for c := 0 to 31 do with display_form[c]
  do begin
          length := 2;
          representation[1] := '''';
          representation[2] := chr(c+64);
     end;
for c := 32 to 126 do with display_form[c]
  do begin
          length := 1;
          representation[1] := chr(c);
     end;
for c := 127 to 130 do with display_form[c]
  do begin
          length := 2;
          representation[1] := '''';
          representation[2] := '_';
     end;

with mode
  do begin
          quit := false;
          skip := false;

          number_check := false;
          mixed_alphanumerics := false;
          ignore_uppers := false;

          correct := false;
          train := false;
          end_of_file := false;

          debug := 0;
     end;
```

```
n_cmd_pool_entries := 0;
table_1_initialize;
table_2_initialize;
table_3_initialize;

for i3 := 0 to max_lines
 do context_buffer[i3].length := 0;

with current_position
  do begin
            line := max_lines;
            column := 0;
      end;

context_is_displayed := false;

char_saved := false;

init_common_words_graph;

pool_bottom := 0;
pool_top := max_str_pool;

for i4 := 0 to max_hsh_tbl
 do hsh_tbl[i4] := null;

n_hsh_chn_entries := 0;

n_dsk_blocks := 0;

for i5 := 1 to n_dsk_buffers
 do with dsk_buff_list[i5]
      do begin
            d_block_number := null;
            if i5 ≠ n_dsk_buffers
               then forword := i5+1
               else forword := 0;
            backward := i5-1;
         end;

with dsk_buff_list[0]
      do begin
            d_block_number := null;
            forword := 1;
            backward := n_dsk_buffers;
         end;

n_cands := 0;
```

```
guess_index := 0;

n_subst_tbl := 0;

mod_file[1] := 'DICMO1.TMP          ';
mod_file[2] := 'DICMO2.TMP          ';

current_mod_file := 0;
mod_file_has_changed := true;

n_new_word := 0;
new_word_buffer[0].link := 0;

n_lines := 1;
n_upper := 0;
n_middle := 1;
n_lower := 0;
begin_middle := 1;
end_middle := 1;


nr_lines := 0;
nr_tokens := 0;
nr_chars := 0;;

nr_found_1 := 0;
nr_found_2 := 0;
nr_found_3 := 0;
nr_not_found := 0;
nr_compare := 0;

nt_lines := 0;
nt_tokens := 0;
nt_chars := 0;

nt_found_1 := 0;
nt_found_2 := 0;
nt_found_3 := 0;
nt_not_found := 0;
nt_compare := 0;

leave_proc ( 17,'init_global_variables          ');
end;
```

```
(* ——————————————————————————————————————————— *)
(*                                                                 *)
(*                                                                 *)
(*          Command Input                                          *)
(*                                                                 *)
(*                                                                 *)
(* ——————————————————————————————————————————— *)
```

```
procedure list_commands (table:  command_table);
var
      p:  cmd_pool_index;
begin
      enter_proc ( 18,'list_commands                    ');
      writeln (TTY);
      writeln (TTY, 'Commands are: ');

      writeln (TTY, '        ', '? (Help)');

      p := table.next;
      while p ≠ null
         do begin
                 write (TTY, '        ');
                 write_token (cmd_pool[p].word);
                 writeln (TTY);
                 p := cmd_pool[p].next;
            end;

      writeln (TTY);
      leave_proc ( 18,'list_commands                    ');
end;
```

```
(* * * * * * * * * * * * * * * * * * * * * * * * * * * * * * * * * *)
```

```
procedure read_command (var token:  token_type; table:  command_table);
var
      c:  char;
      j:  token_index;
      question:  boolean;
begin
      enter_proc ( 19,'read_command                     ');
      repeat
             write (TTY, table.prompt, ' ');
             readln (TTY);

             j := 0;
             question := false;
             while not eoln (TTY)
                   do begin
```

```
                        read (TTY, c);
                        if c = '?'
                            then question := true
                            else if j < max_token_length
                                    then begin
                                            j := j + 1;
                                            token.c[j] := lower_case[ord(c)];
                                        end;
                end;

            if question
                then begin
                        list_commands (table);
                        j := 0;
                    end;

            token.length := j;

        until token.length > 0;
        leave_proc ( 19,'read_command                    ');
    end;

* * * * * * * * * * * * * * * * * * * * * * * * * * * * * * * * * * *)

procedure srch_comand_table (table:  command_table;
                             token:  token_type;
                             var cmd:  command);
var
    p:  cmd_pool_index;
    result:  compare_result;

    prefix:  boolean;
    n_prefix:  cmd_pool_index;
    which_prefix:  cmd_pool_index;
begin
    enter_proc ( 20,'srch_comand_table                    ');
    p := table.next;
    result := less;
    n_prefix := 0;

    while (p ≠ null) and (result ≠ equal)
        do begin

                compare (token, result, cmd_pool[p].word, prefix);

                if prefix
                    then begin
                            n_prefix := n_prefix + 1;
                            which_prefix := p;
                        end;
```

```
                        if result ≠ equal then p := cmd_pool[p].next;
            end;

       cmd := 0;
       if result = equal
          then cmd := cmd_pool[p].number
          else if n_prefix = 0
                  then writeln (TTY, 'Unknown Command.')
                  else if n_prefix = 1
                          then cmd := cmd_pool[which_prefix].number
                          else if n_prefix > 1
                                  then writeln (TTY, 'Ambiguous Command.');

       leave_proc ( 20, 'srch_comand_table                ');
end;

(* * * * * * * * * * * * * * * * * * * * * * * * * * * * * * * * * * * * *)

procedure get_command (var cmd: command; table: command_table);
var
       token: token_type;
begin
       enter_proc ( 21, 'get_command                       ');
       repeat
               read_command (token, table);
               srch_comand_table (table, token, cmd);
       until cmd ≠ 0;
       leave_proc ( 21, 'get_command                       ');
end;

(* ————————————————————————————————————————————— *)
(*                                                                *)
(*                                                                *)
(*          Per File Control                                      *)
(*                                                                *)
(*                                                                *)
(* ————————————————————————————————————————————— *)

procedure get_input_file;
var
       file_name: filename;
begin
       enter_proc ( 22, 'get_input_file                    ');
       write (TTY, 'Input file name: ');

       readln (TTY); read (TTY, file_name);
       reset (INPUT, file_name);
       leave_proc ( 22, 'get_input_file                    ');
end;
```

```
procedure get_output_file;
var
      file_name:  filename;
begin
      enter_proc ( 23,'get_output_file                    ');
      write (TTY, 'Output file name:  ');
      readln (TTY); read (TTY, file_name);
      rewrite (OUTPUT, file_name);
      leave_proc ( 23,'get_output_file                    ');
end;
```

(* *)

```
procedure init_variables_for_these_files;
var
      i:  line_number;
begin
      enter_proc ( 24,'init_variables_for_these_files  ');
      mode.end_of_file := false;
      mode.skip := false;

      context_is_displayed := false;
      for i := 0 to max_lines
       do context_buffer[i].length := 0;

      current_position.line := 0;
      current_position.column := 0;

      char_saved := false;

      nr_lines := 0;
      nr_tokens := 0;
      nr_chars := 0;
      nr_found_1 := 0;
      nr_found_2 := 0;
      nr_found_3 := 0;
      nr_not_found := 0;
      nr_compare := 0;

      leave_proc ( 24,'init_variables_for_these_files  ');
end;
```

(* *)

```
procedure per_file_initialize;
begin
      enter_proc ( 25,'per_file_initialize              ');
      get_input_file;
```

```
        get_output_file;
        init_variables_for_these_files;
        leave_proc ( 25,'per_file_initialize              ');
end;

(* * * * * * * * * * * * * * * * * * * * * * * * * * * * * * * * *)

procedure per_file_conclusion;
begin
        enter_proc ( 26,'per_file_conclusion              ');
        close (INPUT);
        close (OUTPUT);

        writeln (TTY);
        writeln (TTY, 'Done.');
        leave_proc ( 26,'per_file_conclusion              ');
end;

(* ——————————————————————————————————— *)
(*                                                                       *)
(*                                                                       *)
(*            Token Input/Output (Syntax)                                *)
(*                                                                       *)
(*                                                                       *)
(* ——————————————————————————————————— *)

procedure get_input (var c:  pseudo_char);
const
        CR = 13;
        LF = 10;
var
        cc:  char;
begin
        enter_proc ( 27,'get_input                        ');
        if eof(INPUT)
           then c := end_of_file
           else begin
                        read (INPUT, cc);
                        if (ord(cc) ≠ CR) or (ord(INPUT^) ≠ LF)
                           then c := ord(cc)
                           else begin
                                        c := end_of_line;
                                        read (INPUT, cc);
                                end;
                end;

        nr_chars := nr_chars + 1;
        nt_chars := nt_chars + 1;
```

```
        leave_proc ( 27,'get_input                        ');
end;
```

(* *)

```
procedure put_output (c:  pseudo_char);
const
        CR = 13;
        LF = 10;
begin
        enter_proc ( 28,'put_output                        ');
        if c ≠ end_of_file
           then if c ≠ end_of_line
                   then write (output, chr(c))
                   else begin
                             write (output, chr(CR));
                             write (output, chr(LF));
                        end;
        leave_proc ( 28,'put_output                        ');
end;
```

(* *)

```
procedure get_chr_from_input (var c:  pseudo_char);
begin
        enter_proc ( 29,'get_chr_from_input               ');
        if char_saved
           then begin
                     c := saved_character;
                     char_saved := false;
                end
           else get_input (c);
        leave_proc ( 29,'get_chr_from_input               ');
end;
```

```
procedure put_chr_back_in_input (c:  pseudo_char);
begin
        enter_proc ( 30,'put_chr_back_in_input            ');
        char_saved := true;
        saved_character := c;
        leave_proc ( 30,'put_chr_back_in_input            ');
end;
```

(* *)

```
procedure read_line (i:  line_number);
var
      c:  pseudo_char;
      j:  line_index;

      display_length:  0..82 (* max_line_length+2 *);
begin
      enter_proc ( 31,'read_line                              ');
      j := 0;
      display_length := 0;

      repeat
              j := j + 1;
              get_chr_from_input (c);
              display_length := display_length + display_form[c].length;
              context_buffer[i].c[j] := c;

      until (c=end_of_line)
           or (c=end_of_file)
           or (display_length>max_line_length);

      if c = end_of_line
         then begin
                    nr_lines := nr_lines + 1;
                    nt_lines := nt_lines + 1;
                end;

      while display_length > max_line_length
         do begin
                    c := context_buffer[i].c[j];
                    put_chr_back_in_input (c);
                    display_length := display_length - display_form[c].length;
                    j := j - 1;
                end;

      context_buffer[i].length := j;

      leave_proc ( 31,'read_line                           ');
end;

(* * * * * * * * * * * * * * * * * * * * * * * * * * * * * * * * * *)

procedure reset_regions;
var
      i:  line_number;
begin
      enter_proc ( 32,'reset_regions                       ');
      for i := 0 to n_lines-n_middle
         do context_buffer[i] := context_buffer[i+n_middle];
```

```
      for i := n_lines-n_middle+1 to n_lines
        do read_line (i);

      context_is_displayed := false;
      leave_proc ( 32,'reset_regions                      ');
end;
```

(* *)

```
procedure update_current_position;
begin
      enter_proc ( 33,'update_current_position           ');
      with current_position
        do begin
                if column < context_buffer[line].length
                  then column := column + 1
                  else repeat
                            column := 1;

                            if line < end_middle
                              then line := line + 1
                              else begin
                                        reset_regions;
                                        line := begin_middle;
                                   end;
                        until column ≤ context_buffer[line].length;
           end;
      leave_proc ( 33,'update_current_position           ');
end;
```

(* *)

```
procedure get_char_from_context_buffer (var c: pseudo_char);
begin
      enter_proc ( 34,'get_char_from_context_buffer      ');
      update_current_position;
      with current_position
        do c := context_buffer[line].c[column];
      leave_proc ( 34,'get_char_from_context_buffer      ');
end;
```

(* *)

```
procedure put_char_back_in_context_buffer (c: pseudo_char);
begin
      enter_proc ( 35,'put_char_back_in_context_buffer ');
      with current_position
        do column := column - 1;
      leave_proc ( 35,'put_char_back_in_context_buffer ');
end;
```

```
(* * * * * * * * * * * * * * * * * * * * * * * * * * * * * * * * * * * *)


procedure find_non_delimiter (var c:  pseudo_char);
begin
      enter_proc ( 36,'find_non_delimiter                  ');
      while (class[c] = delimiter) and (c ≠ end_of_file)
         do begin
                      put_output (c);
                      get_char_from_context_buffer (c);
               end;
      leave_proc ( 36,'find_non_delimiter                  ');
end;


(* * * * * * * * * * * * * * * * * * * * * * * * * * * * * * * * * * * *)


procedure collect_possible_token (var c:  pseudo_char;
                                  var token:  token_type);
begin
      enter_proc ( 37,'collect_possible_token              ');
      token.length := 0;
      while (class[c] ≠ delimiter) and (token.length < max_token_length)
         do begin
                      token.length := token.length + 1;
                      token.c[token.length] := c;
                      get_char_from_context_buffer (c);
               end;

      (* end of collection; delimiter or too long *)
      leave_proc ( 37,'collect_possible_token              ');
end;


(* * * * * * * * * * * * * * * * * * * * * * * * * * * * * * * * * * * *)


procedure check_class_of_token (var is_token:  boolean; token:  token_type);
var
      cc:  char_class;
      class_set:  array [char_class] of boolean;
      class_type:  0..7 (* bit encoding of class_set *);

      i:  token_index;
begin
      enter_proc ( 38,'check_class_of_token                ');
      for cc := alphabetic to apostrophe do class_set[cc] := false;
      class_type := 0;
```

```
168 i := 1 to token.length
   do if not class_set[class[token.c[i]]]
        then begin
                class_set[class[token.c[i]]] := true;
                class_type := class_type + bit[class[token.c[i]]];
             end;

(* * * * * * * * * * * * * * * * * * * * * * * * * *)

case class_type of

      1 (* alphabetic *):
         is_token := true;

      2 (* numeric *):
         is_token := mode.number_check;

      4 (* apostrophe *):
         is_token := false;

      3 (* alphabetic, numeric *):
         is_token := mode.mixed_alphanumerics;

      5 (* alphabetic, apostrophe *):
         is_token := true;

      6 (* numeric, apostrophe *):
         is_token := mode.number_check
                        and mode.mixed_alphanumerics;

      7 (* alphabetic, numeric, apostrophe *):
         is_token := mode.mixed_alphanumerics;

   end (* case *);

   leave_proc ( 38,'check_class_of_token            ');
end;

* * * * * * * * * * * * * * * * * * * * * * * * * * * * * * * *)

procedure check_all_uppers (var is_token: boolean; token: token_type);
var
      i: token_index;
begin
      enter_proc ( 39,'check_all_uppers            ');
      if mode.ignore_uppers
        then begin
```

```
                          i := token.length;
                          while (i>0) and (upper_or_lower[token.c[i]] ≠ lower)
                             do i := i - 1;
                          is_token := (i = 0);
                 end;
         leave_proc ( 39,'check_all_uppers                    ');
end;
```

(* *)

```
procedure determine_if_token (var is_token: boolean; token: token_type);
begin
        enter_proc ( 40,'determine_if_token                  ');

        if token.length ≥ max_token_length
           then is_token := false (* too long *)
           else begin
                        check_class_of_token (is_token, token);
                        if is_token
                            then check_all_uppers (is_token, token);
                end;
        leave_proc ( 40,'determine_if_token                  ');
end;
```

(* *)

```
procedure copy_to_delimiter (token: token_type; var c: pseudo_char);
var
        i: token_index;
begin
        enter_proc ( 41,'copy_to_delimiter                  ');
         (* output token buffer *)
        for i := 1 to token.length
         do put_output (token.c[i]);

         (* now if token was too long copy to next delimiter *)
        while class[c] ≠ delimiter
           do begin
                        put_output (c);
                        get_char_from_context_buffer (c);
                end;
        leave_proc ( 41,'copy_to_delimiter                  ');
end;
```

(* *)

```
procedure get_token (var token:  token_type);
var
     c:  pseudo_char;
     is_token:  boolean;
begin
     enter_proc ( 42,'get_token                    ');

     get_char_from_context_buffer (c);

     repeat
          find_non_delimiter (c);

          if c = end_of_file
             then begin
                         mode.end_of_file := true;
                         token.length := 0;
                 end
             else begin
                         collect_possible_token (c, token);
                         determine_if_token (is_token, token);
                         if not is_token
                            then copy_to_delimiter (token, c);
                 end;

     until is_token or mode.end_of_file;

     put_char_back_in_context_buffer (c);

     nr_tokens := nr_tokens + 1;
     nt_tokens := nt_tokens + 1;

     leave_proc ( 42,'get_token                    ');
end;

* * * * * * * * * * * * * * * * * * * * * * * * * * * * * * * * * * * *)

procedure output_token (token:  token_type);
var
     j:  token_index;
begin
     enter_proc ( 43,'output_token                 ');
     for j := 1 to token.length
      do put_output (token.c[j]);
     leave_proc ( 43,'output_token                 ');
end;
```

```
(* ——————————————————————————————————————— *)
(*                                                              *)
(*                                                              *)
(*            Modification File Maintenance                     *)
(*                                                              *)
(*                                                              *)
(* ——————————————————————————————————————— *)
```

procedure *set_up_mod_files*;
var
    next: 1..2;
begin
    enter_proc (44,'set_up_mod_files   ');
    if *current_mod_file* = 1
      then *next* := 2
      else *next* := 1;

    if *current_mod_file* = 0
      then *end_of_mod_file* := *true*
      else begin
            reset (*MOD_IN*, *mod_file*[*current_mod_file*]);
            end_of_mod_file := *eof*(*MOD_IN*);
        end;

    rewrite (*MOD_OUT*, *mod_file*[*next*]);
    leave_proc (44,'set_up_mod_files   ');
end;

```
(* * * * * * * * * * * * * * * * * * * * * * * * * * * * * * * * * * *)
```

procedure *put_mod_token* (*srch_tok*: *srch_tok_type*);
const
    CR = 13;
    LF = 10;
var
    j: *token_index*;
begin
    enter_proc (45,'put_mod_token   ');
    for *j* := 1 **to** *srch_tok.length*
     do *write* (*MOD_OUT*, *chr*(*pseudo_code*[*srch_tok.c*[*j*]]));
    write (*MOD_OUT*, *chr*(*CR*));
    write (*MOD_OUT*, *chr*(*LF*));
    leave_proc (45,'put_mod_token   ');
  end;

```
procedure put_mod_string (s:  string);
const
      CR  =  13;
      LF  =  10;
var
      j:  token_index;
      k:  str_pool_index;
begin
      enter_proc ( 46,'put_mod_string                 ');
      k := s.first_char;
      for j := 1 to s.length
       do begin
                k := k + 1;
                write (MOD_OUT, chr(pseudo_code[str_pool[k]]));
           end;

      write (MOD_OUT, chr(CR));
      write (MOD_OUT, chr(LF));
      leave_proc ( 46,'put_mod_string                 ');
end;
```

* *)

```
procedure reset_mod_files;
begin
      enter_proc ( 47,'reset_mod_files                ');
      close (MOD_IN);
      close (MOD_OUT);

      if current_mod_file = 1
         then current_mod_file := 2
         else current_mod_file := 1;

      mod_file_has_changed := true;
      leave_proc ( 47,'reset_mod_files                ');
end;
```

* *)

```
procedure get_next_from_file (var F:  text; var srch_tok:  srch_tok_type;
                              var end_of_file:  boolean);
var
      cc:  char;
      c:  pseudo_char;
      j:  token_index;
begin
      enter_proc ( 48,'get_next_from_file             ');
```

```
      if not end_of_file
        then begin
                  c := null;
                  while (class[c] = delimiter) and not eof(F)
                      do begin
                                read (F, cc);
                                c := ord(cc);
                           end;

                  if eof(F)
                      then end_of_file := true
                      else begin
                                  j := 0;
                                  repeat
                                      j := j + 1;
                                      srch_tok.c[j] := search_code[c];
                                      read (F, cc);
                                      c := ord(cc);
                                  until (class[c]=delimiter) or eof(F);
                                  srch_tok.length := j;
                           end;
              end;
      leave_proc ( 48,'get_next_from_file                   ');
end;
```

```
(* * * * * * * * * * * * * * * * * * * * * * * * * * * * * * * * * *)
```

```
procedure merge_with_modification_file;
var
      p:  new_word_index;
      srch_tok:  srch_tok_type;
      result:  compare_result;
begin
      enter_proc ( 49,'merge_with_modification_file      ');
      set_up_mod_files;
      p := new_word_buffer[0].link;
      get_next_from_file (MOD_IN, srch_tok, end_of_mod_file);
      while (p ≠ null) or not end_of_mod_file
          do begin
                    if p = null
                        then result := less
                        else if end_of_mod_file
                                then result := greater
                                else string_compare (srch_tok, result,
                                                    new_word_buffer[p].word);
```

```
                    case result of

                  less:  begin
                                put_mod_token (srch_tok);
                                get_next_from_file (MOD_IN, srch_tok,
                                                    end_of_mod_file);
                         end;

                 equal:  p := new_word_buffer[p].link;

               greater:  begin
                                put_mod_string (new_word_buffer[p].word);
                                p := new_word_buffer[p].link;
                         end;

                  end (* case *);
                 end;

      reset_mod_files;
      leave_proc ( 49,'merge_with_modification_file      ');
   end;


* * * * * * * * * * * * * * * * * * * * * * * * * * * * * * * * * * * * * *)


procedure reverse_linked_list;
var
      last:  new_word_index;
      p:  new_word_index;
      q:  new_word_index;
begin
      enter_proc ( 50,'reverse_linked_list              ');
      last := 0;
      p := new_word_buffer[last].link (* head *);
      while p ≠ null
         do begin
                q := new_word_buffer[p].link;
                new_word_buffer[p].link := last;
                last := p;
                p := q;
            end;

      new_word_buffer[0].link := last;
      leave_proc ( 50,'reverse_linked_list              ');
   end;


* * * * * * * * * * * * * * * * * * * * * * * * * * * * * * * * * * * * * *)
```

```
procedure flush_new_word_buffer;
begin
      enter_proc ( 51,'flush_new_word_buffer              ');
      if n_new_word > 0
         then begin
                     reverse_linked_list;
                     merge_with_modification_file;
              end;
      n_new_word := 0;
      new_word_buffer[0].link := 0;
      leave_proc ( 51,'flush_new_word_buffer              ');
end;
```

```
(* —————————————————————————————————————————— *)
(*                                                             *)
(*                                                             *)
(*            String Pool Management                           *)
(*                                                             *)
(*                                                             *)
(* —————————————————————————————————————————— *)
```

```
procedure str_pool_overflow;
var
      i:  hsh_tbl_index;
begin
      enter_proc ( 52,'str_pool_overflow              ');

      flush_new_word_buffer;

        (* delete all hash table entries *)

      for i := 0 to max_hsh_tbl
       do hsh_tbl[i] := null;

      n_hsh_chn_entries := 0;

        (* redefine disk index, if necessary *)
      if mod_file_has_changed
         then pool_bottom := 0
         else with dsk_index[n_dsk_blocks].last_word
              do pool_bottom := first_char + length;

      leave_proc ( 52,'str_pool_overflow              ');
end;
```

```
(* * * * * * * * * * * * * * * * * * * * * * * * * * * * * * * * * * *)
```

```
procedure define_low_string (srch_tok:  srch_tok_type; var s:  string);
var
     i:   token_index;
     k:   str_pool_index;
begin
     enter_proc ( 53,'define_low_string                    ');
     if pool_bottom + srch_tok.length > pool_top
        then str_pool_overflow;

     s.length := srch_tok.length;
     s.first_char := pool_bottom;

     k := pool_bottom
     for i := 1 to s.length
       do begin
               k := k + 1;
               str_pool[k] := srch_tok.c[i];
           end;

     pool_bottom := k;
     leave_proc ( 53,'define_low_string                    ');
end;


procedure define_high_string (srch_tok:  srch_tok_type; var s:  string);
var
     i:   token_index;
     k:   str_pool_index;
begin
     enter_proc ( 54,'define_high_string                    ');
     if pool_top - srch_tok.length < pool_bottom
        then str_pool_overflow;

     s.length := srch_tok.length;

     k := pool_top;
     i := s.length;
     while i > 0
        do begin
               str_pool[k] := srch_tok.c[i];
               k := k - 1;
               i := i - 1;
           end;

     pool_top := k;
     s.first_char := pool_top;
     leave_proc ( 54,'define_high_string                    ');
end;
```

```
(* ———————————————————————————————————————— *)
(*                                                              *)
(*                                                              *)
(*         Disk Dictionary Creation                            *)
(*                                                              *)
(*                                                              *)
(* ———————————————————————————————————————— *)
```

procedure *set_up_for_disk_creation* (**var** *end_of_input*: *boolean*);
begin
      enter_proc (55,'set_up_for_disk_creation   ');
      if *current_mod_file* = 0
         then *end_of_mod_file* := *true*
         else begin
                    reset (*MOD_IN*, *mod_file*[*current_mod_file*]);
                    end_of_mod_file := *false*;
                    get_next_from_file(*MOD_IN*,*mod_token*,*end_of_mod_file*);
              end;

      reset (*MASTER*, 'MASTER.DIC');
      end_of_master_file := *false*;
      get_next_from_file (*MASTER*, *master_token*, *end_of_master_file*);

      end_of_input := *end_of_mod_file* **and** *end_of_master_file*;

      rewrite (*DICT*, 'DISK.TMP');
      n_dsk_blocks := 0;
      current_buffer := 1;
      next_in_buffer := 0;
      leave_proc (55,'set_up_for_disk_creation   ');
end;

```
(* * * * * * * * * * * * * * * * * * * * * * * * * * * * * * * * * * * * * *)
```

procedure *get_next_merged_token* (**var** *srch_tok*: *srch_tok_type*;
                               var *end_of_input*: *boolean*);
var
      result: *compare_result*;
begin
      enter_proc (56,'get_next_merged_token   ');
      if *end_of_master_file*
         then if *end_of_mod_file*
             then *end_of_input* := *true*
             else *result* := *less*
         else if *end_of_mod_file*
             then *result* := *greater*
             else *srch_compare* (*mod_token*, *result*, *master_token*);

```
   if not end_of_input
      then case result of
              less:  begin
                        srch_tok := mod_token;
                        get_next_from_file (MOD_IN, mod_token,
                                                    end_of_mod_file);
                     end;

              equal: begin
                        srch_tok := mod_token;
                        get_next_from_file (MOD_IN, mod_token,
                                                    end_of_mod_file);
                        get_next_from_file (MASTER, master_token,
                                                    end_of_master_file);
                     end;

              greater: begin
                        srch_tok := master_token;
                        get_next_from_file (MASTER, master_token,
                                                    end_of_master_file);
                     end;

              end (* case *);
   leave_proc ( 56,'get_next_merged_token             ');
end;


* * * * * * * * * * * * * * * * * * * * * * * * * * * * * * * * * *)

procedure output_disk_block;
var
     i:  0..length_of_dsk_block;
begin
     enter_proc ( 57,'output_disk_block               ');
     define_low_string (last_token, dsk_index[n_dsk_blocks].last_word);

     for i := next_in_buffer to length_of_dsk_block
      do dsk_buffer[current_buffer][i] := null;

     direct_write (n_dsk_blocks, dsk_buffer[current_buffer]);

     dsk_buff_list[current_buffer].d_block_number := n_dsk_blocks;

     current_buffer := 1 + current_buffer mod n_dsk_buffers;
     next_in_buffer := 0;
     leave_proc ( 57,'output_disk_block          ');
end;
```

```
procedure put_token_to_disk_dictionary (srch_tok:  srch_tok_type);
var
      i:  token_index;
begin
      enter_proc ( 58,'put_token_to_disk_dictionary      ');
      if next_in_buffer+srch_tok.length ≥ length_of_dsk_block
         then output_disk_block;

      if next_in_buffer = 0
         then begin
                        n_dsk_blocks := n_dsk_blocks + 1;
                        define_low_string (srch_tok,
                                        dsk_index[n_dsk_blocks].first_word);
              end;
      last_token := srch_tok;

      for i := 1 to srch_tok.length
        do begin
                        dsk_buffer[current_buffer][next_in_buffer] := srch_tok.c[i];
                        next_in_buffer := next_in_buffer + 1;
            end;
      dsk_buffer[current_buffer][next_in_buffer] := 0;
      next_in_buffer := next_in_buffer + 1;
      leave_proc ( 58,'put_token_to_disk_dictionary      ');
end;

(* * * * * * * * * * * * * * * * * * * * * * * * * * * * * * * * * * * * * *)


procedure finish_disk_dictionary_creation;
begin
      enter_proc ( 59,'finish_disk_dictionary_creation ');
      output_disk_block;
      reset (DICT);

      mod_file_has_changed := false;
      close (MOD_IN);
      close (MASTER);
      leave_proc ( 59,'finish_disk_dictionary_creation ');
end;

(* * * * * * * * * * * * * * * * * * * * * * * * * * * * * * * * * * * * * *)


procedure define_disk_dictionary;
var
      end_of_input:  boolean;
      srch_tok:  srch_tok_type;
begin
      enter_proc ( 60,'define_disk_dictionary          ');
```

```
        str_pool_overflow;
        set_up_for_disk_creation (end_of_input);
        while not end_of_input
            do begin
                    get_next_merged_token (srch_tok, end_of_input);
                    if not end_of_input
                        then put_token_to_disk_dictionary (srch_tok);
                end;
        finish_disk_dictionary_creation;
        leave_proc ( 60,'define_disk_dictionary          ');
end;


(*  ———————————————————————————————————————————————  *)
(*                                                     *)
(*                                                     *)
(*                                                     *)
(*              Search Dictionary                      *)
(*                                                     *)
(*                                                     *)
(*                                                     *)
(*  ———————————————————————————————————————————————  *)


procedure srch_comon_words (srch_tok:  srch_tok_type; var found:  boolean);
var
        j:   token_index;
        p:   node_index;
begin
        enter_proc ( 61,'srch_comon_words             ');
        j := 1; (* steps from 1 to srch_tok.length *)
        p := srch_tok.c[j]; (* pointer into node in graph *)

        while (j < srch_tok.length) and (p ≠ null)
            do begin
                    j := j + 1;
                    p := graph[p].next;
                    while (p ≠ null) and (graph[p].c < srch_tok.c[j])
                        do p := graph[p].alt;
                    if graph[p].c ≠ srch_tok.c[j]
                        then p := null;
                end;

        found := (p ≠ null) and graph[p].end_of_word;

        if found
            then begin
                    nr_found_1 := nr_found_1 + 1;
                    nt_found_1 := nt_found_1 + 1;
                end;

        leave_proc ( 61,'srch_comon_words             ');
end;
```

```
(* * * * * * * * * * * * * * * * * * * * * ·* * * * * * * * * * * * * * *)


function hash (srch_tok:  srch_tok_type):  hsh_tbl_index;
begin
        enter_proc ( 62,'hash                              ');
        hash := ( ( (lower_case[srch_tok.c[1]]*29)
                    + lower_case[srch_tok.c[srch_tok.length]]) * 11
                    + srch_tok.length)
                                        mod (max_hsh_tbl + 1);
        leave_proc ( 62,'hash                          ');
end;


(* * * * * * * * * * * * * * * * * * * * * * * * * * * * * * * * * * * *)


procedure search_document_words (srch_tok:  srch_tok_type;
                                 var found:  boolean);
var
        p:  hsh_chn_index;
        result:  compare_result;
begin
        enter_proc ( 63,'search_document_words             ');
        found := false;
        p := hsh_tbl[ hash(srch_tok) ];

        while (p ≠ null) and not found
            do begin
                    (* compare token with word in hash table *)
                    string_compare (srch_tok, result, hsh_chn[p].word);
                    if result = equal
                        then found := true
                        else p := hsh_chn[p].link;
               end;

        if found
            then begin
                    nr_found_2 := nr_found_2 + 1;
                    nt_found_2 := nt_found_2 + 1;
               end;

        leave_proc ( 63,'search_document_words             ');
end;


(* * * * * * * * * * * * * * * * * * * * * * * * * * * * * * * * * * * *)
```

```
procedure add_to_list_of_document_words (srch_tok:  srch_tok_type);
var
     k:  hsh_tbl_index;
     p:  hsh_chn_index;
begin
     enter_proc ( 64,'add_to_list_of_document_words     ');
     (* get hash chain entry *)

     if n_hsh_chn_entries ≥ max_hsh_chn
        then str_pool_overflow
        else begin
                   (* new hash table entry *)
                   n_hsh_chn_entries := n_hsh_chn_entries + 1;
                   p := n_hsh_chn_entries;

                   (* define new word *)
                   define_low_string (srch_tok, hsh_chn[p].word);

                   (* link into hash chain *)
                   k := hash(srch_tok);
                   hsh_chn[p].link := hsh_tbl[k];
                   hsh_tbl[k] := p;
             end;
     leave_proc ( 64,'add_to_list_of_document_words     ');
end;

(* * * * * * * * * * * * * * * * * * * * * * * * * * * * * * * * * * * * *)

procedure find_index_of_dsk_block (srch_tok:  srch_tok_type;
                                   var block_number:  dsk_block_index;
                                   var found:  boolean);
var
     low:  dsk_block_index;
     mid:  dsk_block_index;

     high:  dsk_block_index;
     result:  compare_result;
begin
     enter_proc ( 65,'find_index_of_dsk_block          ');
     found := false;
     block_number := null;

     low := 1;
     high := n_dsk_blocks;

     (* find the block with first[high] < srch_tok < first[high+1] *)
```

```
      while (high ≥ low) and not found
         do begin
                    mid := (high+low) div 2;

                    string_compare (srch_tok,result,dsk_index[mid].first_word);
                    case result of

                         less:   high := mid - 1;
                      greater:   low := mid + 1;
                        equal:   begin
                                        block_number := null;
                                        found := true;
                                    end;
                    end (* case *);

             end (* while *);

      if not found and (high>0)
         then begin  (* check if  first[high] < srch_tok < last[high] *)

                    string_compare (srch_tok,result, dsk_index[high].last_word);

                    case result of

                         less:   block_number := high;
                      greater:   block_number := null;
                        equal:   begin
                                        block_number := null;
                                        found := true;
                                    end;
                    end (* case *);

             end;
      leave_proc ( 65,'find_index_of_dsk_block            ');
end;

(* * * * * * * * * * * * * * * * * * * * * * * * * * * * * * * * * * * *)

procedure get_dsk_block (j:  dsk_block_index; var i:  dsk_buff_index);
begin
      enter_proc ( 66,'get_dsk_block                  ');
      (* search to see if block j already in a buffer *)

      i := 0;
      repeat
             i := i + 1;
      until (i≥ n_dsk_buffers) or (dsk_buff_list[i].d_block_number = j);
```

```
if dsk_buff_list[i].d_block_number ≠ j
    then begin
                (* not in a buffer now, pick LRU and read into it *)
                i := dsk_buff_list[0].backward;
                dsk_buff_list[i].d_block_number := j;
                direct_read (j, dsk_buffer[i]);
        end;

(* block j is in buffer i *)

if dsk_buff_list[i].backward ≠ 0
    then begin
                (* take buffer i out of doubly-linked list *)
                dsk_buff_list[dsk_buff_list[i].backward].forword :=
                                                dsk_buff_list[i].forword;
                dsk_buff_list[dsk_buff_list[i].forword].backward :=
                                                dsk_buff_list[i].backward;

                (* put at front of list *)
                dsk_buff_list[i].forword := dsk_buff_list[0].forword;
                dsk_buff_list[i].backward := 0;

                dsk_buff_list[dsk_buff_list[i].forword].backward := i;
                dsk_buff_list[0].forword := i;
        end;

    leave_proc ( 66,'get_dsk_block                      ');
end;

(* * * * * * * * * * * * * * * * * * * * * * * * * * * * * * * * * * * *)

procedure search_dsk_block (srch_tok:  srch_tok_type;
                            block_number:  dsk_block_index;
                            var found:  boolean);
var
    i:  dsk_buff_index;
    j:  token_index;
    k:  0..length_of_dsk_block;

begin
    enter_proc ( 67,'search_dsk_block                   ');
    get_dsk_block (block_number, i);

    found := false;
    k := 0;
    repeat
```

```
            j := 1;
            while (srch_tok.c[j] = dsk_buffer[i][k])
                    and (j ≤ srch_tok.length)
                do begin
                            j := j + 1;
                            k := k + 1;
                    end;

            if (j = srch_tok.length+1) and (dsk_buffer[i][k]=null)
                then found := true
                else begin (* get on to next word *)
                            while dsk_buffer[i][k] ≠ null
                                do k := k + 1;
                            while (dsk_buffer[i][k]=null)
                                    and (k < length_of_dsk_block)
                                do k := k + 1;
                    end;

    until found or (k ≥ length_of_dsk_block);
    leave_proc ( 67,'search_dsk_block                  ');
end;
```

```
(* * * * * * * * * * * * * * * * * * * * * * * * * * * * * * * * * * *)
```

```
procedure search_disk_dictionary (srch_tok:  srch_tok_type;
                                var found:  boolean);
var
    block_number:  dsk_block_index;
begin
    enter_proc ( 68,'search_disk_dictionary             ');
    if mod_file_has_changed
        then define_disk_dictionary;

    found := false;
    find_index_of_dsk_block (srch_tok, block_number, found);
    if not found and (block_number ≠ null)
        then search_dsk_block (srch_tok, block_number, found);

    if found
        then begin
                    nr_found_3 := nr_found_3 + 1;
                    nt_found_3 := nt_found_3 + 1;
            end;

    leave_proc ( 68,'search_disk_dictionary             ');
end;
```

```
(* * * * * * * * * * * * * * * * * * * * * * * * * * * * * * * * * * *)
```

```
procedure search_dictionary (token:  token_type; var found:  boolean);
var
      srch_tok:  srch_tok_type;
begin
      enter_proc ( 69,'search_dictionary                    ');
      found := false;

      translate_for_search (token, srch_tok);

      if srch_tok.length > 0
         then begin
              srch_comon_words (srch_tok, found);
              if not found
                 then begin
                      search_document_words (srch_tok, found);
                      if not found
                         then begin
                              search_disk_dictionary (srch_tok, found);
                              if found
                              then add_to_list_of_document_words(srch_tok);
                           end;
                   end;
            end;

      if not found
         then begin
                      nr_not_found := nr_not_found + 1;
                      nt_not_found := nt_not_found + 1;
               end;


      leave_proc ( 69,'search_dictionary                    ');
end;
```

```
(* ————————————————————————————————————————— *)
(*                                                                *)
(*                                                                *)
(*            Local Dictionary Management                         *)
(*                                                                *)
(*                                                                *)
(*                                                                *)
(* ————————————————————————————————————————— *)
```

```
procedure insert_sorted (srch_tok:  srch_tok_type);
var
      p:  new_word_index;
      last:  new_word_index;
      result:  compare_result;
```

```
begin
        enter_proc ( 70,'insert_sorted                          ');
        p := 0;
        repeat
                last := p;
                p := new_word_buffer[p].link;
                if p = null
                    then result := greater
                    else string_compare (srch_tok, result,
                                            new_word_buffer[p].word);
        until (result ≠ less);

        if result = greater
          then begin
                    n_new_word := n_new_word + 1;
                    define_low_string (srch_tok,
                        new_word_buffer[n_new_word].word);
                    new_word_buffer[n_new_word].link := p;
                    new_word_buffer[last].link := n_new_word;
                end;

        leave_proc ( 70,'insert_sorted                          ');
end;

(* * * * * * * * * * * * * * * * * * * * * * * * * * * * * * * * * * * * *)

procedure add_to_new_word_buffer (token:  token_type);
var
        srch_tok:  srch_tok_type;
begin
        enter_proc ( 71,'add_to_new_word_buffer                 ');

        if n_new_word ≥ max_new_word
            then str_pool_overflow;
        translate_for_search (token, srch_tok);
        add_to_list_of_document_words (srch_tok);
        insert_sorted (srch_tok);

        leave_proc ( 71,'add_to_new_word_buffer                 ');
end;

(* * * * * * * * * * * * * * * * * * * * * * * * * * * * * * * * * * * * *)

procedure clear_new_word_buffer;
begin
        enter_proc ( 72,'clear_new_word_buffer                  ');
        n_new_word := 0;
        new_word_buffer[0].link := 0;
        leave_proc ( 72,'clear_new_word_buffer                  ');
end;
```

```
(* * * * *  * * * * * * * * * * * * * * * * * * * * * * * * * * * *)

procedure clear_local_dictionary;
begin
      enter_proc ( 73,'clear_local_dictionary                  ');
      if (current_mod_file ≠ 0) or (n_new_word ≠ 0)
         then mod_file_has_changed := true;

      current_mod_file := 0;
      clear_new_word_buffer;
      leave_proc ( 73,'clear_local_dictionary                  ');
end;

(* * * * * * * * * * * * * * * * * * * * * * * * * * * * * * * * * *)

procedure dump_local_dictionary;
var
      c:  char;
      file_name:  filename;
begin
      enter_proc ( 74,'dump_local_dictionary                   ');
      str_pool_overflow;

      write (TTY, 'Output file name:  ');
      readln (TTY); read (TTY, file_name);
      rewrite (MOD_OUT, file_name);

      if current_mod_file ≠ 0
         then begin
                     reset (MOD_IN, mod_file[current_mod_file]);
                     while not eof(MOD_IN)
                        do begin
                                 read (MOD_IN, c);
                                 write (MOD_OUT, c);
                           end;
                     close (MOD_IN);
               end;

      close (MOD_OUT);
      leave_proc ( 74,'dump_local_dictionary                   ');
end;

(* * * * * * * * * * * * * * * * * * * * * * * * * * * * * * * * * *)

procedure collect_user_token (var c:  pseudo_char; var token:  token_type);
var
      j:  token_index;
      cc:  char;
```

```
begin
        enter_proc ( 75,'collect_user_token                    ');
        j := 0;
        while (class[c] ≠ delimiter) and (j < max_token_length)
            do begin
                        j := j + 1;
                        token.c[j] := c;

                        if eof(USER)
                            then c := end_of_file
                             else begin
                                        read (USER, cc);
                                        c := ord(cc);
                                    end;
                end;

        if class[c] = delimiter
            then token.length := j
            else begin
                        token.length := 0;
                        while class[c] ≠ delimiter
                            do if eof(USER)
                                    then c := end_of_file
                                    else begin
                                                read (USER, cc);
                                                c := ord(cc);
                                        end;
                end;

        leave_proc ( 75,'collect_user_token                    ');
end;

(* * * * * * * * * * * * * * * * * * * * * * * * * * * * * * * * * * * *)

procedure load_local_dictionary;
var
        token:  token_type;
        c:  pseudo_char;
        cc:  char;
        file_name:  filename;
begin
        enter_proc ( 76,'load_local_dictionary                    ');
        write (TTY, 'Load file name:  ');
        readln (TTY); read (TTY, file_name);
        reset (USER, file_name);
```

```
        while not eof(USER)
           do begin
                  repeat
                        read (USER, cc);
                        c := ord(cc);
                  until eof(USER) or not (class[c] = delimiter);

                  if not eof(USER)
                     then begin
                            collect_user_token (c, token);
                            if token.length > 0
                               then add_to_new_word_buffer (token);

                        end;
             end;

        close (USER);
        leave_proc ( 76,'load_local_dictionary             ');
   end;


(* ————————————————————————————————————————— *)
(*                                                               *)
(*                                                               *)
(*         Spelling Correction                                   *)
(*                                                               *)
(*                                                               *)
(* ————————————————————————————————————————— *)

procedure new_cand (token:  token_type);
begin
     enter_proc ( 77,'new_cand                        ');
     if n_cands < max_cand_list_length
        then begin
                  n_cands := n_cands + 1;
                  cand[n_cands] := token;
              end;
     leave_proc ( 77,'new_cand                        ');
end;


(* * * * * * * * * * * * * * * * * * * * * * * * * * * * * * * *)

procedure try_one_letter_wrong_at (i:  token_index; new_token:  token_type);
var
     old_c:  pseudo_char;
     c:  pseudo_char;
     found:  boolean;
```

```
begin
        enter_proc ( 78,'try_one_letter_wrong_at                ');
        old_c := new_token.c[i];

        for c := ord('a') to ord('z')
          do if c ≠ old_c
                then begin
                                new_token.c[i] := c;
                                search_dictionary (new_token, found);
                                if found
                                     then new_cand (new_token);
                        end;

        new_token.c[i] := old_c;  (* restore *)
        leave_proc ( 78,'try_one_letter_wrong_at                ');
end;


(* * * * * * * * * * * * * * * * * * * * * * * * * * * * * * * * * * * * *)


procedure try_transposed_letters (token:   token_type);
var
        c:  pseudo_char;
        i:  token_index;
        new_token:  token_type;
        found:  boolean;
begin
        enter_proc ( 79,'try_transposed_letters           ');
        new_token := token;

        (* exchange letters *)
        i := 1;
        c := new_token.c[1];

        while i < token.length
          do begin
                        new_token.c[i] := new_token.c[i+1];
                        new_token.c[i+1] := c;

                        search_dictionary (new_token, found);
                        if found
                           then new_cand (new_token);

                        (* generate next token *)
                        i := i + 1;
                        c := new_token.c[i-1];
                        new_token.c[i-1] := new_token.c[i];
                end;
        leave_proc ( 79,'try_transposed_letters           ');
end;
```

```
(* * * * * * * * * * * * * * * * * * * * * * * * * * * * * * * * *)

procedure try_extra_letter (token:  token_type);
var
      i:  token_index;
      new_token:  token_type;
      found:  boolean;
begin
      enter_proc ( 80,'try_extra_letter                  ');
      for i := 1 to token.length - 1
       do new_token.c[i] := token.c[i+1];
      new_token.length := token.length - 1;

      for i := 1 to token.length
       do begin
                search_dictionary (new_token, found);
                if found
                   then new_cand (new_token);

                new_token.c[i] := token.c[i];
           end;
      leave_proc ( 80,'try_extra_letter                  ');
end;

(* * * * * * * * * * * * * * * * * * * * * * * * * * * * * * * * *)

procedure try_wrong_letter (token:  token_type);
var
      i:  token_index;
      new_token:  token_type;

begin
      enter_proc ( 81,'try_wrong_letter                  ');
      new_token := token;

      for i := 1 to new_token.length
       do try_one_letter_wrong_at (i, new_token);

      leave_proc ( 81,'try_wrong_letter                  ');
end;

(* * * * * * * * * * * * * * * * * * * * * * * * * * * * * * * * *)

procedure try_missing_letter (token:  token_type);
var
      i:  token_index;
      new_token:  token_type;
```

```
begin
        enter_proc ( 82,'try_missing_letter                    ');
        new_token.length := token.length + 1;
        for i := 1 to token.length
         do new_token.c[i+1] := token.c[i];

        for i := 1 to new_token.length
         do begin
                    new_token.c[i] := null;
                    try_one_letter_wrong_at (i, new_token);
                    if i < new_token.length
                        then new_token.c[i] := token.c[i];
             end;
        leave_proc ( 82,'try_missing_letter                    ');
end;

(* * * * * * * * * * * * * * * * * * * * * * * * * * * * * * * * * * *)
procedure display_guess;
begin
        enter_proc ( 83,'display_guess                     ');
        if guess_index ≠ 0
           then begin
                    write (TTY, 'I guess:  ');
                    display_token (cand[guess_index]);
                    writeln (TTY);
                end;
        leave_proc ( 83,'display_guess                     ');
end;


procedure guess_correct_spelling;
begin
        enter_proc ( 84,'guess_correct_spelling            ');
        if n_cands = 1
           then guess_index := 1
           else guess_index := 0;

        leave_proc ( 84,'guess_correct_spelling            ');
end;

(* * * * * * * * * * * * * * * * * * * * * * * * * * * * * * * * * * *)

procedure find_cands (token:  token_type);
begin
        enter_proc ( 85,'find_cands                      ');
        n_cands := 0;
```

```
        try_transposed_letters (token);
        try_extra_letter (token);
        try_wrong_letter (token);
        try_missing_letter (token);

        guess_correct_spelling;
        leave_proc ( 85,'find_cands                        ');
end;

(* ————————————————————————————————————————— *)
(*                                                              *)
(*                                                              *)
(*          User Options and Commands                           *)
(*                                                              *)
(*                                                              *)
(* ————————————————————————————————————————— *)

procedure list_modes;
begin
        enter_proc ( 86,'list_modes                         ');
        writeln (TTY);
        writeln (TTY, 'Current Mode is:');
        writeln (TTY);

        if mode.number_check
           then writeln (TTY, 'Numbers are checked.');
        if mode.mixed_alphanumerics
           then writeln (TTY, 'Mixed letters and numbers are checked.');
        if mode.ignore_uppers
           then writeln (TTY, 'Strictly upper-case words are not checked.');

        if mode.quit
           then writeln (TTY, 'About to abort session')
        else if mode.skip
           then writeln (TTY, 'About to skip to end-of-file')
        else if mode.correct
           then writeln (TTY, 'Checking and correcting.')
           else writeln (TTY, 'Checking for misspellings.');

        if mode.train
           then writeln (TTY, '   Training mode.');

        if mode.debug ≠ 0
           then writeln (TTY, '   Debug mode ', mode.debug:3);

        leave_proc ( 86,'list_modes                         ');
end;
```

```
(* * * * * * * * * * * * * * * * * * * * * * * * * * * * * * * * * * * *)


procedure set_modes;
var
      cmd:   command;
      quit:  boolean;
      i:   integer;
begin
      enter_proc ( 87,'set_modes                              ');
      repeat
            quit := false;

            get_command (cmd, table_3);

            case cmd of
              1 (* help *):  list_commands (table_3);
              2 (* quit *):  quit := true;
              3 (* skip *):  mode.skip := true;
              4 (* train *):  mode.train := true;
              5 (* notrain *):  mode.train := false;
              6 (* number *):  mode.number_check := true;
              7 (* nonumber *):  mode.number_check := false;
              8 (* mixed *):  mode.mixed_alphanumerics := true;
              9 (* nomixed *):  mode.mixed_alphanumerics := false;
             10 (* uppers *):  mode.ignore_uppers := false;
             11 (* nouppers *):  mode.ignore_uppers := true;
             12 (* correct *):  mode.correct := true;
             13 (* check *):  mode.correct := false;
             14 (* list *):  list_modes;
             15 (* debug *):  begin
                                  repeat
                                        write (TTY, 'Debug level:   ');
                                        readln (TTY);
                                        read (TTY, i);
                                  until (0 ≤ i)
                                        and (i ≤ max_proc_level);
                                  mode.debug := i;
                              end;

            end (* case *);

      until quit;
      leave_proc ( 87,'set_modes                              ');
end;


(* * * * * * * * * * * * * * * * * * * * * * * * * * * * * * * * * * * *)
```

```
procedure define_context;
begin
        enter_proc ( 88,'define_context                    ');
        repeat (* until legal values *)

                repeat
                        write (TTY, 'Size of upper region:  ');
                        readln (TTY); read (TTY, n_upper);
                until n_upper ≥ 0;

                repeat
                        write (TTY, 'Size of middle region:  ');
                        readln (TTY); read (TTY, n_middle);
                until n_middle ≥ 0;

                repeat
                        write (TTY, 'Size of lower region:  ');
                        readln (TTY); read (TTY, n_lower);
                until n_lower ≥ 0;

                if n_upper+n_middle+n_lower > max_lines
                    then writeln (TTY, 'Total context exceeds ',
                                 max_lines:4, ' lines.');

        until n_upper+n_middle+n_lower ≤ max_lines;

        if n_middle = 0
           then if n_lower > 0
                    then begin
                                n_lower := n_lower -1;
                                n_middle := 1;
                         end
                else if n_upper > 0
                        then begin
                                n_upper := n_upper -1;
                                n_middle := 1;
                             end;

        n_lines := n_upper+n_middle+n_lower;

        if n_lines = 0
           then begin_middle := 0
           else begin_middle := n_upper+1;

        end_middle := begin_middle + n_middle;
        leave_proc ( 88,'define_context                    ');
end;
```

(* *)

```
procedure write_statistics;
var
      file_name:  filename;
      i:   proc_number;
      j:   proc_number;
begin
      enter_proc ( 89,'write_statistics                    ');

      writeln (TTY);
      write (TTY, nr_chars:6, ' characters read  ');
      writeln (TTY, '(', nt_chars:6, ')');
      write (TTY, nr_tokens:6, ' tokens read       ');
      writeln (TTY, '(', nt_tokens:6, ')');
      write (TTY, nr_lines:6, ' lines read        ');
      writeln (TTY, '(', nt_lines:6, ')');

      writeln (TTY);
      write (TTY, n_hsh_chn_entries:6,' hash table entries   ');
      writeln (TTY, '(', max_hsh_chn:6, ' maximum)');
      write (TTY, n_new_word:6,          ' inserted words        ');
      writeln (TTY, '(', max_new_word:6, ' maximum)');
      write (TTY, n_subst_tbl:6,          ' sub table entries    ');
      writeln (TTY, '(', max_subst_tbl:6, ' maximum)');
      write (TTY, pool_top-pool_bottom:6, ' left in string pool  ');
      writeln (TTY, '(', max_str_pool:6, ' maximum)');


      writeln (TTY);
      write (TTY, nr_found_1:6, ' tokens found in graph         ');
      writeln (TTY, '(', nt_found_1:6, ')');
      write (TTY, nr_found_2:6, ' tokens found in hash table ');
      writeln (TTY, '(', nt_found_2:6, ')');
      write (TTY, nr_found_3:6, ' tokens found on disk          ');
      writeln (TTY, '(', nt_found_3:6, ')');
      write (TTY, nr_not_found:6, ' tokens not found             ');
      writeln (TTY, '(', nt_not_found:6, ')');
      write (TTY, nr_compare:6, ' compares                     ');
      writeln (TTY, '(', nt_compare:6, ')');

      writeln (TTY);
      write (TTY, 'File for statistics:  ');
      readln (TTY); read (TTY, file_name);
      rewrite (USER, file_name);

      writeln (USER);
```

```
       for i := 1 to max_proc_number
        do if proc_i_calls[i] ≠ 0
               then begin
                         write (USER, proc_name[i]);
                         writeln (USER, proc_i_calls[i]);

                         writeln (USER, '    from');
                         for j := 1 to max_proc_number
                          do if proc_ij_calls[i][j] ≠ 0
                                then begin
                                          write (USER, chr(9), proc_name[j]);
                                          writeln (USER, proc_ij_calls[i][j]);
                                     end;
                         writeln (USER);
               end;

     leave_proc ( 89,'write_statistics              ');
end;

* * * * * * * * * * * * * * * * * * * * * * * * * * * * * * * * *)

procedure insert_token (token:  token_type);
begin
     enter_proc ( 90,'insert_token                  ');
     add_to_new_word_buffer (token);
     leave_proc ( 90,'insert_token                  ');
end;

* * * * * * * * * * * * * * * * * * * * * * * * * * * * * * * * *)

procedure edit_context;
begin
     enter_proc ( 91,'edit_context                  ');
     writeln (TTY, 'Not Implemented Yet');
     leave_proc ( 91,'edit_context                  ');
end;

* * * * * * * * * * * * * * * * * * * * * * * * * * * * * * * * *)

procedure list_cands;
var
     i:  cand_table_index;
begin
     enter_proc ( 92,'list_cands                    ');
     if n_cands ≤ 0
        then writeln (TTY, 'No candidates found')
        else for i := 1 to n_cands
                do begin
```

```
                              write (TTY, i:4, '   ');
                              display_token (cand[i]);
                              writeln (TTY);
                      end;
        guess_index := 0;
        leave_proc ( 92,'list_cands                          ');
end;

(* * * * * * * * * * * * * * * * * * * * * * * * * * * * * * * * * * *)


procedure replace_with_cand (var token:  token_type;
                                        var complete:  boolean);
begin
        enter_proc ( 93,'replace_with_cand                  ');
        if guess_index = 0
            then begin
                      write (TTY, 'Which candidate number? ');
                      readln (TTY); read (TTY, guess_index);
                end;

        if (0 < guess_index) and (guess_index ≤ n_cands)
            then token := cand[guess_index]
            else complete := false;
        leave_proc ( 93,'replace_with_cand                  ');
end;

(* * * * * * * * * * * * * * * * * * * * * * * * * * * * * * * * * * * *)


procedure read_new_token (var new_token:  token_type);
var
        j:  token_index;
        c:  char;
begin
        enter_proc ( 94,'read_new_token                    ');
        j := 0;

        readln (TTY);
        while not eoln (TTY)
            do begin
                      j := j + 1;
                      read (TTY, c);
                      new_token.c[j] := ord(c);
                end;
        new_token.length := j;
        leave_proc ( 94,'read_new_token                    ');
end;

(* * * * * * * * * * * * * * * * * * * * * * * * * * * * * * * * * * * *)
```

```
procedure replace_token (var token:  token_type);
var
      new_token:  token_type;
begin
      enter_proc ( 95,'replace_token                        ');
      write (TTY, 'Replace with:  ');
      read_new_token (new_token);
      token := new_token;
      leave_proc ( 95,'replace_token                        ');
end;
```

(* *)

```
procedure remember (old:  token_type; new:  token_type);
var
      srch_tok:  srch_tok_type;
begin
      enter_proc ( 96,'remember                           ');
      n_subst_tbl := n_subst_tbl + 1;

      translate_for_search (old, srch_tok);
      define_high_string (srch_tok, subst_tbl[n_subst_tbl].old);

      translate_for_search (new, srch_tok);
      define_high_string (srch_tok, subst_tbl[n_subst_tbl].new);
      leave_proc ( 96,'remember                           ');
end;


procedure substitute_token (var token:  token_type);
var
      new_token:  token_type;
begin
      enter_proc ( 97,'substitute_token                   ');

      write (TTY, 'Substitute throughout with:  ');
      read_new_token (new_token);
      remember (token, new_token);
      token := new_token;
      leave_proc ( 97,'substitute_token                   ');
end;
```

```
(* ———————————————————————————————————————————— *)
(*                                                              *)
(*                                                              *)
(*              Top-Level Control                               *)
(*                                                              *)
(*                                                              *)
(* ———————————————————————————————————————————— *)
```

```
procedure search_subst_tbl (token:  token_type;
                            var i:  subst_tbl_index;
                            var found:  boolean);
var
     srch_tok:  srch_tok_type;
     result:  compare_result;
begin
     enter_proc ( 98,'search_subst_tbl                    ');
     translate_for_search (token, srch_tok);
     i := n_subst_tbl;
     found := false;
     while (0 < i) and not found
         do begin
                 string_compare (srch_tok, result, subst_tbl[i].old);
                 if result = equal
                     then found := true
                     else i := i - 1;
             end;
     leave_proc ( 98,'search_subst_tbl                 ');
end;
```

```
(* * * * * * * * * * * * * * * * * * * * * * * * * * * * * * * * * * * * *)
```

```
procedure check_for_generated_command (var token:  token_type;
                                       var complete:  boolean);
var
     i:  subst_tbl_index;
     found:  boolean;
begin
     enter_proc ( 99,'check_for_generated—command      ');
     complete := false;

     search_subst_tbl (token, i, found);
     if found
         then begin
                 complete := true;
                 change_to_pseudo (subst_tbl[i].new, token);
             end;

     if not complete and mode.train
         then begin
                 insert_token (token);
                 complete := true;
             end;

     leave_proc ( 99,'check_for_generated_command      ');
end;
```

```
(* * * * * * * * * * * * * * * * * * * * * * * * * * * * * * * * * *)

procedure do_table_2_command (var token:  token_type);
var
      complete:  boolean;
      cmd:  command;
begin
      enter_proc (100,'do_table_2_command                    ');

      repeat (* until complete *)

              get_command (cmd, table_2);
              complete := true;

              case cmd of

                      1 (* help *):  begin
                                              list_commands (table_2);
                                              complete := false;
                                          end;

                      2 (* quit *):  mode.quit := true;

                      3 (* skip *):  mode.skip := true;

                      4 (* accept *):  begin (* no action necessary *) end;

                      5 (* insert *):  insert_token (token);

                      6 (* replace *):  replace_token (token);

                      7 (* substitute *):  substitute_token (token);

                      8 (* edit *):  edit_context;

                      9 (* clear *):  begin
                                              clear_local_dictionary;
                                              complete := false;
                                          end;

                      10 (* load *):  begin
                                              load_local_dictionary;
                                              complete := false;
                                          end;

                      11 (* dump *):  begin
                                              dump_local_dictionary;
                                              complete := false;
                                          end;
```

```
                12 (* mode *):  begin
                                    set_modes;
                                    complete := false;
                            end;

                13 (* display *):  begin
                                        context_is_displayed := false;
                                        display_context;
                                        display_token (token);
                                        writeln (TTY, ' ?');
                                        display_guess;
                                        complete := false;
                                    end;

                14 (* correct *):  replace_with_cand (token, complete);

                15 (* list *):  begin
                                    list_cands;
                                    complete := false;
                            end;

                16 (* statistics *):  begin
                                        write_statistics;
                                        complete := false;
                                    end;

            end (* case *);

        until complete;

        leave_proc (100,'do_table_2_command              ');
end;

(* * * * * * * * * * * * * * * * * * * * * * * * * * * * * * * * * * * * * *)

procedure ask_user_about_it (var token:  token_type);
var
        complete:  boolean;
begin
        enter_proc (101,'ask_user_about_it              ');
        check_for_generated_command (token, complete);

        if not complete
            then begin
                    guess_index := 0;
```

```
                    if mode.correct
                        then find_cands (token);

                    display_context;
                    display_token (token);
                    writeln (TTY, ' ?');
                    display_guess;

                    do_table_2_command (token);
            end;
        leave_proc (101,'ask_user_about_it               ');
end;
```

(* *)

```
procedure check_spelling;
var
        token:  token_type;
        found:  boolean;
begin
        enter_proc (102,'check_spelling                 ');
        per_file_initialize;

        repeat
                get_token (token);

                if not mode.skip and not mode.end_of_file
                    then begin
                                search_dictionary (token, found);

                                if not found
                                    then ask_user_about_it (token);
                        end;

                output_token (token);

        until mode.end_of_file or mode.quit;

        per_file_conclusion;
        leave_proc (102,'check_speling                  ');
end;
```

(* *)

```
procedure execute_table_1_command (cmd:  command);
begin
        enter_proc (103,'execute_table_1_command           ');
```

```
        case cmd of

                1 (* help *):  list_commands (table_1);

                2 (* quit *):  mode.quit := true;

                3 (* check *):  begin
                                        mode.correct := false;
                                        check_spelling;
                                end;

                4 (* correct *):  begin
                                        mode.correct := true;
                                        check_spelling;
                                end;

                5 (* clear *):  clear_local_dictionary;

                6 (* load *):  load_local_dictionary;

                7 (* dump *):  dump_local_dictionary;

                8 (* mode *):  set_modes;

                9 (* statistics *):  write_statistics;

                10 (* context *):  define_context;


        end (* case *);

        leave_proc (103,'execute_table_1_command          ');
end;

(* * * * * * * * * * * * * * * * * * * * * * * * * * * * * * * * * * * *)

procedure do_speller_directive;
var
        cmd:  command;
begin
        enter_proc (104,'do_speller_directive           ');
        get_command (cmd, table_1);
        execute_table_1_command (cmd);
        leave_proc (104,'do_speller_directive           ');
end;
```

```
(* ————————————————————————————————————————————— *)
(*                                                               *)
(*                                                               *)
(*           Main Program                                        *)
(*                                                               *)
(*                                                               *)
(* ————————————————————————————————————————————— *)
```

begin
      init_global_variables;

      repeat
              do_speller_directive;
      until *mode.quit*;

end.

INDEX